PRACTICE
MAKES
PERFECT™

Multiplication
AND
Division

Multiplication
AND
Division

Judith A. Muschla and Gary Robert Muschla

New York   Chicago   San Francisco   Lisbon   London   Madrid   Mexico City
Milan   New Delhi   San Juan   Seoul   Singapore   Sydney   Toronto

*The **McGraw-Hill** Companies*

Copyright © 2012 by Judith A. Muschla and Gary Robert Muschla. All rights reserved.
Printed in the United States of America. Except as permitted under the United States
Copyright Act of 1976, no part of this publication may be reproduced or distributed in
any form or by any means, or stored in a database or retrieval system, without the prior
written permission of the publisher.

1 2 3 4 5 6 7 8 9 10 11 12 13 14 15 16 17   QDB/QDB   1 9 8 7 6 5 4 3 2

ISBN   978-0-07-177285-3
MHID   0-07-177285-5

e-ISBN   978-0-07-178111-4
e-MHID   0-07-178111-0

Library of Congress Control Number 2011936573

Trademarks: McGraw-Hill, the McGraw-Hill Publishing logo, Practice Makes Perfect,
and related trade dress are trademarks or registered trademarks of The McGraw-Hill
Companies and/or its affiliates in the United States and other countries and may not
be used without written permission. All other trademarks are the property of their
respective owners. The McGraw-Hill Companies is not associated with any product or
vendor mentioned in this book.

Interior design by Nick Panos

McGraw-Hill products are available at special quantity discounts to use as premiums
and sales promotions or for use in corporate training programs. To contact a
representative, please e-mail us at bulksales@mcgraw-hill.com.

This book is printed on acid-free paper.

Contents

About This Book

Multiplication and division are basic mathematical operations. When students acquire the skills for multiplying and dividing, they also acquire an important sense of numbers and their relationships.

Practice Makes Perfect: Multiplication and Division is a useful resource for learning multiplication and division skills as they apply to whole numbers, decimals, fractions, and positive and negative numbers. The book is composed of skill sheets and self-correcting worksheets, and it may be used by both students and teachers. Students (working alone or with their parents) can study the skill sheets and complete the worksheets, while teachers will find the materials of the book useful for classroom instruction.

Learning the skills for proficient multiplication and division can be challenging for many students. It is our hope that this book will help students master these skills in an interesting and enjoyable manner.

How to Use This Book

Practice Makes Perfect: Multiplication and Division is divided into eight parts. Each part includes skill sheets and self-correcting worksheets that are based on typical math curricula for grades 4 through 8. An answer key is included at the end of the book.

Part 1 "Multiplying Whole Numbers," includes 10 skill sheets and 15 worksheets that focus on basic multiplication facts, multiples, properties of multiplication, multiplying one-, two-, three-, and four-digit numbers, estimation, and exponents. A review worksheet concludes the part.

Part 2 "Dividing Whole Numbers," includes 11 skill sheets and 18 worksheets that focus on basic division facts, factors, prime and composite numbers, dividing by one-, two-, and three-digit divisors, estimation, and divisibility rules. A review worksheet concludes the part.

Part 3 "Multiplying Decimals," includes four skill sheets and 10 worksheets that address multiplying whole numbers by decimals, multiplying decimals by decimals, and estimation. A review worksheet ends the part.

Part 4 "Dividing Decimals," includes six skill sheets and 12 worksheets that focus on dividing decimals by whole numbers, dividing decimals by decimals with one-, two-, and three-digit divisors, and estimation. A review worksheet concludes the part.

Part 5 "Multiplying Fractions," includes seven skill sheets and 11 worksheets on simplifying fractions, renaming mixed numbers and improper fractions, multiplying whole numbers and fractions, multiplying fractions and mixed numbers, and estimation. A review worksheet ends the part.

Part 6 "Dividing Fractions," includes eight skill sheets and 12 worksheets on dividing whole numbers and fractions, dividing fractions and mixed numbers, estimation, simplifying complex fractions, expressing fractions as terminating or repeating decimals, and changing decimals to fractions. A review worksheet concludes the section.

Part 7 "Multiplying Signed Numbers," includes four skill sheets and six worksheets on multiplying positive and negative integers, simplifying positive and negative integers with exponents, and multiplying positive and negative rational numbers. A review worksheet ends the part.

Part 8 "Dividing Signed Numbers," includes three skill sheets and five worksheets that focus on dividing positive and negative integers, dividing positive and negative rational numbers, and dividing positive and negative rational numbers with exponents. A review worksheet concludes the part.

The skill sheets and worksheets throughout the book are designed to make learning multiplication and division easy and enjoyable. Each skill sheet serves as a resource that contains step-by-step instructions for mastering a specific skill, examples, and practice problems. The worksheets have easy-to-follow directions and require no additional materials. We suggest that you study a skill sheet before beginning a worksheet that follows it. If you need help in completing the worksheet, refer back to the information on the skill sheet.

The worksheets are self-correcting. You are presented with a trivia-type question at the top of the worksheet, which you can answer by completing the problems on the worksheet correctly. You will find that some skills are addressed by two, three, or more worksheets. In such cases, the worksheets progress in degree of difficulty from basic to more challenging. For some worksheets, you will need to solve the problems on a separate sheet of paper. Because this book is designed to help build your multiplication and division skills, you should solve the problems without using a calculator.

The skill sheets and worksheets provide 150 activities. Together they offer a rich resource of material that will help you master the skills to multiply and divide with confidence and accuracy.

Multiplying Whole Numbers

Multiplication is a mathematical operation that can be thought of as repeated addition. Rather than adding to find the total number of equal-sized groups, you can multiply to find the total number. The numbers being multiplied are called factors. The answer to a multiplication problem is called the product. Multiplication is the inverse, or opposite, operation of division.

Multiplying Whole Numbers

Multiplication Facts

Multiplication can be thought of as repeated addition. When you have two or more groups that have the same number of items, you can multiply to find how many items you have in all.

Suppose you have 3 sets of 4.

☐☐☐☐ ☐☐☐☐ ☐☐☐☐

You can find the total number of items in the sets by adding 4 + 4 + 4 = 12, or you can multiply 3 × 4 = 12.

The multiplication table below contains basic multiplication facts. Knowing these facts will help you to multiply numbers. Study the table until you remember the facts.

×	0	1	2	3	4	5	6	7	8	9	10
0	0	0	0	0	0	0	0	0	0	0	0
1	0	1	2	3	4	5	6	7	8	9	10
2	0	2	4	6	8	10	12	14	16	18	20
3	0	3	6	9	12	15	18	21	24	27	30
4	0	4	8	12	16	20	24	28	32	36	40
5	0	5	10	15	20	25	30	35	40	45	50
6	0	6	12	18	24	30	36	42	48	54	60
7	0	7	14	21	28	35	42	49	56	63	70
8	0	8	16	24	32	40	48	56	64	72	80
9	0	9	18	27	36	45	54	63	72	81	90
10	0	10	20	30	40	50	60	70	80	90	100

Practice
Find the products.

1. 9 × 3 = _____
2. 7 × 6 = _____
3. 3 × 5 = _____
4. 4 × 4 = _____
5. 8 × 2 = _____
6. 4 × 9 = _____
7. 10 × 6 = _____
8. 6 × 0 = _____

1.1 Arithmetic

The word *arithmetic* comes from the Greek word *arithetike*. What was the original meaning of *arithetike*?

To answer the question, find the products. Match each answer to one of the answer choices in the list after the problems. Then write the letter that corresponds to each answer in the space above its problem number at the bottom of the page. Some answers will be used more than once. Some answers will not be used. You will need to divide the letters into words.

1. $8 \times 2 =$ _____   2. $0 \times 3 =$ _____   3. $4 \times 3 =$ _____

4. $9 \times 6 =$ _____   5. $9 \times 4 =$ _____   6. $8 \times 3 =$ _____

7. $5 \times 5 =$ _____   8. $6 \times 4 =$ _____   9. $7 \times 5 =$ _____

10. $7 \times 7 =$ _____   11. $4 \times 7 =$ _____   12. $7 \times 6 =$ _____

13. $9 \times 8 =$ _____   14. $6 \times 2 =$ _____   15. $5 \times 0 =$ _____

16. $3 \times 8 =$ _____

Answer Choices

42 H	0 O	21 S	49 E	12 N	16 R	81 M
36 C	24 T	72 F	28 U	35 I	48 L	25 A
29 W	54 G					

___ ___ ___ ___ ___ ___ ___ ___ ___ ___ ___ ___ ___ ___ ___ ___
 6   12 10   7   1   8   2 13   5 15 11   3 16   9 14   4

Multiples, Common Multiples, and Least Common Multiples

The answer to a multiplication problem is called a product. A multiple is a product of a whole number and another whole number.

Following are the first 10 multiples of 3 and the first 10 multiples of 5.

3 × 1 = 3	5 × 1 = 5
3 × 2 = 6	5 × 2 = 10
3 × 3 = 9	5 × 3 = 15
3 × 4 = 12	5 × 4 = 20
3 × 5 = 15	5 × 5 = 25
3 × 6 = 18	5 × 6 = 30
3 × 7 = 21	5 × 7 = 35
3 × 8 = 24	5 × 8 = 40
3 × 9 = 27	5 × 9 = 45
3 × 10 = 30	5 × 10 = 50

You will see that 15 and 30 are multiples of both 3 and 5. They are called common multiples. The least, or smallest, common multiple of 3 and 5 is 15.

If you know your multiplication facts well, you can skip count to find multiples.

For example, by skip counting the basic multiplication facts of 2 you will find 2, 4, 6, 8, 10, 12, 14, 16, 18, and 20. These are also the first 10 multiples of 2.

If you skip count the basic multiplication facts of 7, you will find 7, 14, 21, 28, 35, 42, 49, 56, 63, and 70. These are also the first 10 multiples of 7.

Practice

1. List the first 10 multiples of 4 and the first 10 multiples of 6.

2. Find the first three common multiples of 4 and 6, and the least common multiple.

1.2 A Cartoon Star

In Italy, this famous cartoon star is known as Topolino. Who is he?

To answer the question, read each statement below. If the statement is correct, write the letter for **correct** in the space above its number at the bottom of the page. If the statement is incorrect, write the letter for **incorrect**. You will need to divide the letters into words.

1. A common multiple of 3 and 4 is 12.
   E. correct   **I.** incorrect

2. The least common multiple of 3 and 6 is 18.
   U. correct   **O.** incorrect

3. Common multiples of 5 and 7 are 25 and 35.
   A. correct   **I.** incorrect

4. The least common multiple of 2 and 9 is 18.
   E. correct   **N.** incorrect

5. A common multiple of 6 and 8 is 48.
   K. correct   **T.** incorrect

6. Common multiples of 5 and 6 are 30 and 45.
   R. correct   **M.** incorrect

7. A multiple of 8 is 64.
   S. correct   **U.** incorrect

8. The least common multiple of 4 and 5 is 20.
   Y. correct   **R.** incorrect

9. The first five multiples of 4 are 4, 8, 16, 24, and 32.
   D. correct   **M.** incorrect

10. A multiple of 7 is 21.
    U. correct   **E.** incorrect

11. The only multiple of 1 and 2 is 0.
    F. correct   **C.** incorrect

___ ___ ___ ___ ___ ___ ___ ___ ___ ___ ___
 9   3   11   5   1   8   6   2   10   7   4

Properties of Multiplication

In math, a property is a rule. Understanding the properties below can help you to multiply.

- **Commutative property:** Factors (the numbers to be multiplied) can be multiplied in any order without changing the product (answer).

  $3 \times 4 = 4 \times 3$ The product is 12.

- **Associative property:** Factors can be grouped in any way without changing the product.

  $(2 \times 5) \times 4 = 2 \times (5 \times 4)$ The product is 40.

  Note that parentheses are a grouping symbol. Operations in parentheses must be done first. In the example $(2 \times 5) \times 4$, 2×5 is in parentheses and must be multiplied first. The product is 10, which is then multiplied by 4. In the example $2 \times (5 \times 4)$, 5×4 is in parentheses and must be multiplied first. The product is 20, which is then multiplied by 2. In both cases the product is 40.

- **Distributive property:** Multiplying a sum by a factor is the same as multiplying each number in the sum by the factor, and then adding the products.

  $2 \times 25 = 2 \times (20 + 5) = (2 \times 20) + (2 \times 5)$ The product is 50.

- **Property of 1:** The product of any factor and 1 is the factor.

  $8 \times 1 = 8$ and $1 \times 5 = 5$

- **Property of 0:** The product of any factor and 0 is 0.

  $6 \times 0 = 0$ and $0 \times 3 = 0$

Practice
Name the property each example illustrates.

1. $(4 \times 8) \times 2 = 4 \times (8 \times 2)$ _____

2. $7 \times 0 = 0$ _____

3. $9 \times 2 = 2 \times 9$ _____

4. $6 \times (4 + 7) = (6 \times 4) + (6 \times 7)$ _____

5. $6 \times 1 = 6$ _____

1.3 A Big Bug

This giant dragonfly lived about 300 million years ago. With a wingspan of about 29 inches (the size of a hawk), it is thought to be the largest insect ever to have lived on Earth. What was its name?

  To answer the question, match the property with its example. Choose your answers from the examples below each property. Write the letter that corresponds to each answer in the space above its problem number at the bottom of the page.

1. Property of 0
   I $7 \times 1 = 7$ **E** $8 \times 0 = 0$

2. Associative property
   A $4 \times (3 + 2) = (4 \times 3) + (4 \times 2)$ **E** $3 \times (4 \times 2) = (3 \times 4) \times 2$

3. Property of 1
   R $1 \times 8 = 8$ **T** $3 \times (4 + 2)$

4. Commutative property
   G $3 \times 4 = 4 \times 3$ **P** $3 \times (4 \times 6) = (3 \times 4) \times 6$

5. Distributive property
   S $(6 \times 3) \times 2 = 6 \times (3 \times 2)$ **N** $3 \times (5 + 2) = (3 \times 5) + (3 \times 2)$

6. Associative property
   T $4 \times (5 + 6)$ **M** $(9 \times 4) \times 3 = 9 \times (4 \times 3)$

7. Property of 1
   O $4 \times 1 = 4$ **E** $4 \times 4 = (8 \times 2)$

8. Commutative property
   I $2 \times (4 \times 5) = (2 \times 5) \times (2 \times 4)$ **N** $9 \times 3 = 3 \times 9$

9. Property of 0
   S $5 \times 1 = 1 \times 5$ **U** $0 \times 5 = 0$

10. Distributive property
   A $7 \times (5 + 2) = (7 \times 5) + (7 \times 2)$ **I** $(3 \times 4) \times 2 = 3 \times (4 \times 2)$

$$\underline{\quad} \ \underline{\quad} \ \underline{\quad} \ \underline{\quad} \ \underline{\quad} \ \underline{\quad} \ \underline{\quad} \ \underline{\quad} \ \underline{\quad} \ \underline{\quad}$$
$$\ \ 6 \quad 2 \quad 4 \quad 10 \quad 8 \quad 1 \quad 9 \quad 3 \quad 7 \quad 5$$

Multiplying by One-Digit Numbers

When you multiply, you must multiply the digits one place at a time.

```
  32
×  8
```
Multiply 8 ones × 2 ones to find 16 ones.

```
  1
  32
×  8
   6
```
Regroup because 16 ones = 1 ten and 6 ones.
Place 6 ones in the ones column.
Place 1 ten in the tens column above the 3 tens.

```
  1
  32
×  8
 256
```
Multiply 8 ones × 3 tens to find 24 tens.
Add the 1 ten to the 24 tens to find 25 tens.

Here are some more examples. The first example does not require regrouping.

```
                5           3 2          4  4
   51          46          286         3,807
×   7         × 9         ×   4         ×     6
  357         414         1,144        22,842
```

Practice
Find the products.

1.   50
   × 4

2.   95
   × 6

3.   253
   × 8

4.   2,642
   × 5

5.   35,706
   × 4

1.4 Kansas

The name Kansas comes from a word of the Sioux, a Native American tribe. What was the original meaning of this word?

To answer the question, find the products. Match each answer to one of the answer choices in the list after the problems. Then write the letter that corresponds to each answer in the space above its problem number at the bottom of the page. Some answers will be used more than once. One answer will not be used. Some letters are provided. You will need to divide the letters into words.

1. 84 × 7	2. 33 × 5	3. 67 × 8	4. 48 × 7	5. 55 × 3
6. 348 × 3	7. 134 × 4	8. 522 × 2	9. 303 × 6	10. 196 × 3
11. 5,274 × 5	12. 7,568 × 6	13. 3,091 × 4	14. 5,628 × 8	15. 8,061 × 4

Answer Choices

165 E	32,244 O	45,408 W	588 H	336 S	1,144 J
45,024 F	1,818 I	536 T	1,044 P	26,370 D	12,364 L

```
__  __  O   __  __  __  O   __  __  __  E
 8   5       6  13   2      14   3  10

__  __  U   __  __  __  __  N   __
 4  15       7   1  12   9      11
```

Multiplying by 10, 100, or 1,000

You can multiply by 10, 100, or 1,000 by multiplying the digits one place at a time.

$$
\begin{array}{r}
27 \\
\times\ 10 \\
\hline
270
\end{array}
$$

Multiply 0×7 ones to find 0.
Multiply 1 ten $\times$ 7 ones to find 7 tens or 70.
Multiply 1 ten $\times$ 2 tens to find 20 tens or 200.
$200 + 70 = 270$

Here is a shortcut.

- To multiply any whole number by 10, write the whole number and add 1 zero.

$$
\begin{array}{r}
24 \\
\times\ 10 \\
\hline
240
\end{array}
$$

The whole number is 24. Add 1 zero for 240.

- To multiply any whole number by 100, write the whole number and add 2 zeros.

$$
\begin{array}{r}
534 \\
\times\ 100 \\
\hline
53{,}400
\end{array}
$$

The whole number is 534. Add 2 zeros for 53,400.

- To multiply any whole number by 1,000, write the whole number and add 3 zeros.

$$
\begin{array}{r}
762 \\
\times\ 1{,}000 \\
\hline
762{,}000
\end{array}
$$

The whole number is 762. Add 3 zeros for 762,000.

Follow this pattern, and add 4 zeros to the whole number when multiplying by 10,000, 5 zeros when multiplying by 100,000, 6 zeros when multiplying by 1,000,000, and so on.

Practice

Find the products. Use the shortcut.

1.	2.	3.	4.	5.
45	87	375	692	735
× 10	× 10	× 100	× 100	× 1,000

1.5 The Government of the United States

The federal government has three branches. What are they?

To answer the question, find the products. Match each answer to one of the answer choices in the list after the problems. Then write the letter that corresponds to each answer in the space above its problem number at the bottom of the page. Some answers will not be used.

1.   36
   × 10

2.   89
   × 10

3.   342
   × 10

4.   706
   × 10

5.   948
  × 100

6.   387
  × 100

7.   529
  × 100

8.   407
  × 100

9.   218
  × 100

10.   735
  × 100

11.   953
  × 1,000

12. 1,675
 × 1,000

13. 1,920
 × 1,000

Answer Choices

1,920,000 E	52,900 V	360 G	5,290 M	7,060 A
890 D	40,700 I	73,500 L	953,000 T	1,675,000 J
38,700 S	3,420 C	95,300 N	94,800 U	21,800 X

___ ___ ___ ___ ___ ___ ___ ___ ___
13   9   13   3   5   11   8   7   13

___ ___ ___ ___ ___ ___ ___ ___ ___ ___ ___
10   13   1   8   6   10   4   11   8   7   13

___ ___ ___ ___ ___ ___ ___ ___
12   5   2   8   3   8   4   10

Multiplying by Multiples of 10, 100, or 1,000

Multiplying by a multiple of 10, 100, or 1,000 is similar to multiplying by 10, 100, or 1,000.

$$
\begin{array}{r}
64 \\
\times\ 30 \\
\hline
0
\end{array}
$$

Multiply 0×4 ones to find 0.

$$
\begin{array}{r}
1 \\
64 \\
\times\ 30 \\
\hline
20
\end{array}
$$

Multiply 3 tens $\times$ 4 ones to find 12 tens.
Regroup because 12 tens = 120 or 1 hundred and 2 tens.
Place the 2 tens in the tens column.
Place the 1 hundred over the hundreds column.

$$
\begin{array}{r}
1 \\
64 \\
\times\ 30 \\
20 \\
1900 \\
\hline
1,920
\end{array}
$$

Multiply 3 tens $\times$ 6 tens to find 18 hundreds.
Add the 1 hundred to the 18 hundreds to find 19 hundreds
or 1,900.
$1,900 + 20 = 1,920$

Here is a shortcut. To multiply a number by a multiple of 10, place a zero in the product and then multiply the number by the number of tens. Remember to regroup if necessary.

$$
\begin{array}{r}
48 \\
\times\ 20 \\
\hline
960
\end{array}
$$

After placing the zero, the process is the same as multiplying 48×2.

This shortcut also works for multiples of 100, 1,000, and so on. For example, when multiplying by a multiple of 100, place 2 zeros in the product and then multiply. When multiplying by a multiple of 1,000, place 3 zeros in the product and then multiply.

Here are some more examples.

$$
\begin{array}{rrrr}
58 & 67 & 972 & 5,266 \\
\times\ 30 & \times\ 40 & \times\ 700 & \times\ 6,000 \\
\hline
1,740 & 2,680 & 680,400 & 31,596,000
\end{array}
$$

Practice
Find the products.

1. $\begin{array}{r} 47 \\ \times\ 60 \\ \hline \end{array}$
2. $\begin{array}{r} 250 \\ \times\ 80 \\ \hline \end{array}$
3. $\begin{array}{r} 783 \\ \times\ 200 \\ \hline \end{array}$
4. $\begin{array}{r} 880 \\ \times\ 600 \\ \hline \end{array}$
5. $\begin{array}{r} 7,561 \\ \times\ 5,000 \\ \hline \end{array}$

1.6 A Poem in Honor of Paul Revere

This American poet wrote the famous poem "Paul Revere's Ride." Who was the poet?

To answer the question, find the products. Match each answer to one of the answer choices in the list after the problems. Then write the letter that corresponds to each answer in the space above its problem number at the bottom of the page. One answer will not be used.

1.   95
    × 30

2.   72
    × 60

3.   84
    × 40

4.   246
    × 50

5.   587
    × 30

6.   972
    × 30

7.   534
    × 60

8.   340
    × 90

9.   684
    × 200

10.   496
    × 700

11.   259
    × 800

12.   740
    × 600

13.   5,238
    × 4,000

14.   8,421
    × 5,000

Answer Choices

4,320 A	42,105,000 L	30,600 G	136,800 N	3,360 T
33,600 C	207,200 F	20,952,000 W	29,160 R	12,300 H
32,040 S	17,610 D	444,000 O	2,850 E	347,200 Y

___ ___ ___ ___ ___   ___ ___ ___ ___ ___ ___ ___ ___ ___
 4   1   9   6 10   13 2 5 7 13 12 6 3 4

___ ___ ___ ___ ___ ___ ___ ___ ___ ___
 14 12 9 8 11 1 14 14 12 13

Multiplying by Two-Digit Numbers

When multiplying by two-digit numbers, you must first multiply by the ones digit, and then multiply by the tens digit.

$$
\begin{array}{r}
5\,2 \\
384 \\
\times\ 46 \\
\hline
2304
\end{array}
$$

Multiply each digit of the first factor by 6 ones.
Regroup as necessary.
$384 \times 6 = 2{,}304$. This is called a partial product.

$$
\begin{array}{r}
3\,1 \\
384 \\
\times\ 46 \\
\hline
2304 \\
15360
\end{array}
$$

Multiply each digit of the first factor by 4 tens.
Write this number under the partial product
found in step 1.
Regroup as necessary.
$384 \times 40 = 15{,}360$. This is also a partial product. (You may omit the zero, which is a placeholder.)

$$
\begin{array}{r}
384 \\
\times\ 46 \\
\hline
2304 \\
15360 \\
\hline
17{,}664
\end{array}
$$

Add the partial products. $2{,}304 + 15{,}360 = 17{,}664$

Here are more examples. The first two show zero as a placeholder in the partial product. The next three omit the placeholder in the partial product.

$\begin{array}{r}32\\ \times\ 71\\ \hline 32\\ 2240\\ \hline 2{,}272\end{array}$	$\begin{array}{r}46\\ \times\ 58\\ \hline 368\\ 2300\\ \hline 2{,}668\end{array}$	$\begin{array}{r}153\\ \times\ 73\\ \hline 459\\ 1071\\ \hline 11{,}169\end{array}$	$\begin{array}{r}537\\ \times\ 24\\ \hline 2148\\ 1074\\ \hline 12{,}888\end{array}$	$\begin{array}{r}906\\ \times\ 62\\ \hline 1812\\ 5436\\ \hline 56{,}172\end{array}$

Practice

Find the products.

1. $\begin{array}{r}241\\ \times\ 27\\ \hline\end{array}$
2. $\begin{array}{r}75\\ \times\ 38\\ \hline\end{array}$
3. $\begin{array}{r}168\\ \times\ 42\\ \hline\end{array}$
4. $\begin{array}{r}218\\ \times\ 53\\ \hline\end{array}$
5. $\begin{array}{r}305\\ \times\ 69\\ \hline\end{array}$

1.7 Stinky Defenses

Skunks are well known for using scent glands for defense. But some other common mammals also use scent glands when attacked or frightened. What animals are these?

To answer the question, find the products. Match each answer to one of the answer choices in the list after the problems. Then write the letter that corresponds to each answer in the space above its problem number at the bottom of the page. Some answers will be used more than once. Some answers will not be used. Some letters are provided.

1. 32 × 72	2. 74 × 27	3. 69 × 86	4. 36 × 64	5. 50 × 84

6. 35 × 57	7. 80 × 39	8. 69 × 96	9. 26 × 93	10. 87 × 79

11. 416 × 38	12. 450 × 47	13. 537 × 53	14. 208 × 76	15. 384 × 89

Answer Choices

2,418 K	4,200 M	22,150 J	1,978 T	21,150 F
30,120 B	28,461 L	3,120 N	15,808 O	2,314 C
5,934 S	6,724 U	1,998 I	2,304 E	6,873 X
1,995 V	34,176 W	6,624 R		

```
__  __  N  __       __  __  __  E  __
 5   2     9        12  14  10     3

__  __  __  __  __  __  I  __  __  S
15  11  13   6   4   8      7   1
```

1.8 The White House Library

This president and his first wife started the library at the White House. Who was he?

To answer the question, find if the product of each problem is correct. If the given product is correct, write the letter for **correct** in the space above its problem number at the bottom of the page. If the given product is incorrect, write the letter for **incorrect**.

1. 75
    × 62
    4,657

    U. correct
    I. incorrect

2. 47
    × 88
    4,135

    N. correct
    E. incorrect

3. 94
    × 28
    2,632

    I. correct
    O. incorrect

4. 68
    × 49
    3,332

    A. correct
    R. incorrect

5. 98
    × 67
    6,566

    L. correct
    U. incorrect

6. 175
    × 45
    7,870

    O. correct
    L. incorrect

7. 207
    × 37
    7,659

    D. correct
    R. incorrect

8. 348
    × 52
    19,096

    S. correct
    O. incorrect

9. 532
    × 63
    33,516

    F. correct
    H. incorrect

10. 695
    × 82
    56,980

    O. correct
    R. incorrect

11. 509
    × 26
    13,334

    O. correct
    L. incorrect

12. 299
    × 56
    16,845

    O. correct
    R. incorrect

13. 302
    × 87
    26,274

    M. correct
    W. incorrect

14. 5,143
    × 32
    164,576

    L. correct
    R. incorrect

15. 6,805
    × 54
    368,470

    S. correct
    M. incorrect

___ ___ ___ ___ ___ ___ ___   ___ ___ ___ ___ ___ ___ ___ ___
13 3 11 6 4 10 7   9 1 14 5 15 8 12 2

Multiplying Whole Numbers

1.9 One-of-a-Kind State

Every state in the United States except one is subdivided into counties. What is the name of this state and what is it subdivided into?

To answer the question, find the products. Match each answer to one of the answer choices in the list after the problems. Then write the letter that corresponds to each answer in the space above its problem number at the bottom of the page. Some answers will be used more than once. One answer will not be used. Some letters are provided.

1.	218	2.	496	3.	168	4.	288	5.	336
	× 23		× 36		× 42		× 62		× 21

6.	205	7.	576	8.	5,648	9.	2,504	10.	2,824
	× 67		× 31		× 24		× 75		× 48

11.	4,294	12.	6,172	13.	7,275	14.	62,308	15.	37,846
	× 85		× 57		× 39		× 78		× 46

Answer Choices

7,056 **S**	364,990 **O**	5,014 **R**	13,735 **E**	351,804 **P**
4,860,024 **U**	283,725 **L**	187,800 **N**	130,735 **T**	
1,740,916 **H**	135,552 **I**	17,856 **A**		

__ __ __ __ __ I __ __ __   __ __ __ __ __ __ __ S

13 11 14 8 5   4 9 2   12 7 1 10 3 15 6

© Judith A. Muschla and Gary Robert Muschla

Multiplying by Two-, Three-, and Four-Digit Numbers

When multiplying large numbers, you must multiply one place at a time.

```
  3 4
  546
× 267
 3822
```
Multiply each digit of the first factor by 7 ones.
Regroup as necessary.
546 × 7 = 3,822

```
  2 3
  546
× 267
 3822
 3276
```
Multiply each digit of the first factor by 6 tens.
Write this partial product under the partial
product found in step 1.
Regroup as necessary.
546 × 60 = 32,760. The zero, which is a placeholder, was
omitted in the second partial product. Be sure to line up the
partial products according to place.

```
   1
   546
 × 267
  3822
  3276
  1092
145,782
```
Multiply each digit of the first factor by 2 hundreds.
Regroup as necessary.
546 × 200 = 109,200
Line up the partial products according to place.
The placeholders (zeros) in the partial products
were omitted.
Add the partial products. 3,822 + 32,760 + 109,200 =
145,782

Here are more examples. The placeholders in the partial products have been omitted.

```
    272          608          398            398            5,812
  ×  54        × 537        × 406   OR     × 406          × 4,735
   1088         4256         2388           2388           29060
   1360         1824          000           1592           17436
  14,688        3040         1592          161,588         40684
              326,496       161,588                        23248
                                                        27,519,820
```

Practice
Find the products.

```
1.    245      2.    240      3.    675      4.    2,084      5.    3,481
    × 582          × 293          × 502          ×  783          × 6,207
```

© Judith A. Muschla and Gary Robert Muschla

1.10 A Wise Man of Ancient Greece

Thales of Miletus was a Greek philosopher and mathematician. What title is Thales known by?

To answer the question, find the products. Match each answer to one of the answer choices in the list after the problems. Then write the letter that corresponds to each answer in the space above its problem number at the bottom of the page. Some answers will be used more than once. Some answers will not be used. One letter is provided. You will need to divide the letters into words.

1.	426	2.	752	3.	328	4.	502	5.	656
	× 93		× 45		× 84		× 65		× 42

6.	292	7.	146	8.	926	9.	649	10.	572
	× 240		× 480		× 286		× 473		× 463

11.	2,066	12.	4,936	13.	4,132	14.	7,853	15.	2,468
	× 648		× 742		× 324		× 3,006		× 1,484

Answer Choices

70,080 R	32,630 A	39,618 G	1,338,768 F	33,840 H
23,606,118 M	264,836 O	306,977 Y	27,552 E	
23,616,118 L	3,662,512 T	316,977 N		

```
                                      E
___ ___ ___ ___ ___ ___ ___ ___ ___      ___ ___ ___ ___ ___ ___
11   4   12  2   3   6   10  13  1        8   14  5   15  7   9
```

1.11 The Great Barrier Reef

Located off the coast of Australia, the Great Barrier Reef is more than 1,200 miles (1,930 km) long. It is a very special place on our planet. Why is the Great Barrier Reef so special?

To answer the question, find the products. Match each answer to one of the answer choices in the list after the problems. Then write the letter that corresponds to each answer in the space above its problem number at the bottom of the page. One answer will not be used.

1.	253 × 86	2.	406 × 39	3.	738 × 45	4.	7,403 × 63	5.	8,246 × 58

6.	627 × 309	7.	421 × 452	8.	254 × 430	9.	1,309 × 275	10.	1,625 × 426

11.	5,821 × 783	12.	6,805 × 703	13.	4,212 × 3,782

Answer Choices

4,783,915 S	193,743 C	109,220 H	21,758 U	33,210 E
15,834 R	359,975 A	466,389 G	190,292 T	478,268 I
4,557,843 N	11,093,594 D	692,250 V	2,127,208 W	
15,929,784 L				

__ __ __ __ __ __ __   __ __ __ __ __ __
13 9 2 4 3 12 7   13 5 10 5 11 4

__ __ __ __ __ __ __ __ __   __ __   __ __ __
12 7 2 1 6 7 1 2 3   5 11   7 8 3

__ __ __
12 3 9

1.12 Florida

The name Florida comes from a Spanish word. What was the original meaning of *Florida*?

To answer the question, find if the product of each problem is correct. If the given product is correct, write the letter for **correct** in the space above its problem number at the bottom of the page. If the given product is incorrect, write the letter for **incorrect**. You will need to divide the letters into words.

1.	2.	3.	4.	5.
615	326	432	509	919
× 34	× 25	× 56	× 24	× 67
20,919	8,150	25,192	12,218	61,573

U. correct   A. correct   I. correct   M. correct   S. correct
O. incorrect   E. incorrect   O. incorrect   F. incorrect   N. incorrect

6.	7.	8.	9.	10.
517	325	245	690	247
× 305	× 728	× 582	× 218	× 549
167,685	236,600	142,590	150,320	135,603

H. correct   E. correct   S. correct   R. correct   E. correct
T. incorrect   S. incorrect   O. incorrect   F. incorrect   H. incorrect

11.	12.	13.	14.
5,218	6,527	1,256	8,273
× 426	× 395	× 3,407	× 2,465
2,222,868	2,578,162	4,279,292	20,392,945

W. correct   T. correct   E. correct   L. correct
U. incorrect   F. incorrect   R. incorrect   S. incorrect

___ ___ ___ ___ ___ ___ ___ ___ ___ ___ ___ ___ ___ ___
12 10 2 8 6 3 9 4 14 1 11 7 13 5

1.13 Sailing South

In 1773, English sea captain James Cook led an expedition to the southern seas. He and his crew became the first Europeans to cross this line of latitude. What line of latitude did Cook and his crew cross?

To answer the question, find if the product of each problem is correct. If the given product is correct, write the letter for **correct** in the space above its problem number at the bottom of the page. If the given product is incorrect, write the letter for **incorrect**. You will need to divide the letters into words.

1. 238	2. 532	3. 608	4. 834	5. 247
× 36	× 72	× 41	× 69	× 84
8,668	38,504	24,928	58,546	20,748

| I. correct | P. correct | I. correct | E. correct | E. correct |
| R. incorrect | R. incorrect | T. incorrect | T. incorrect | N. incorrect |

6. 451	7. 424	8. 603	9. 916	10. 829
× 218	× 421	× 716	× 642	× 508
98,318	178,504	430,748	580,072	421,132

| C. correct | C. correct | P. correct | R. correct | L. correct |
| R. incorrect | A. incorrect | I. incorrect | N. incorrect | R. incorrect |

11. 7,596	12. 6,509	13. 13,052	14. 23,475	15. 25,268
× 1,305	× 3,251	× 6,218	× 4,007	× 3,492
9,922,780	21,160,749	81,157,336	94,064,325	88,225,856

| O. correct | O. correct | A. correct | C. correct | P. correct |
| T. incorrect | C. incorrect | T. incorrect | A. incorrect | A. incorrect |

___ ___ ___ ___ ___ ___ ___ ___ ___ ___ ___ ___ ___ ___
13 9 4 15 1 6 11 3 7 14 8 2 12 10 5

Estimating Products

When you are able to estimate products, you can easily tell if your answer to a multiplication problem is reasonable.

Here is an example. Joe multiplied 378 × 206 and found the product to be 9,828. But his answer was incorrect, because he did not line up the numbers in the partial products correctly. If he had estimated his answer, he would have seen that the product he found was too small.

```
    378                    378
  × 206                  × 206
   2268                   2268
    756  ← Incorrect       756   ← Correct (The zeros as place-
  9,828                  77,868       holders were omitted.)
```

Follow these steps to estimate products:

1. Round each factor.

   378 can be rounded to 400.

   206 can be rounded to 200.

2. Multiply.
```
       400
     × 200
    80,000
```

Based on his estimate, Joe's product of 9,828 is too low. It is not a reasonable answer.

Here are more examples with their estimates.

```
   92 →    90        676 →    700       421 →    400
 × 26 →  × 30      × 38 →  × 40      × 277 →  × 300
          2,700             28,000            120,000
```

Practice
Find the products first. Then estimate to see if your answers are reasonable.

```
1.    85      2.   812     3.   869     4.   265     5.   572
    × 32         × 43        × 19        × 389       × 526
```

1.14 The Top of the World

Because the Earth is tilted on its axis, the sun never sets during the summer in the Arctic. This region of the world is often referred to by a special name. What is this name?

To answer the question, estimate the products. Match each answer to one of the answer choices that follows each problem. Then write the letter that corresponds to each answer in the space above its problem number at the bottom of the page. You will need to divide the letters into words.

1. 92 × 84	2. 32 × 79	3. 184 × 62	4. 110 × 18	5. 196 × 13

| 7,200 E | 2,400 D | 20,000 S | 200 M | 20,000 N |
| 720 I | 24,000 R | 12,000 F | 2,000 G | 2,000 H |

. . . .

6. 194 × 33	7. 210 × 23	8. 293 × 48	9. 407 × 95	10. 316 × 19

| 6,000 U | 40,000 A | 11,600 U | 36,000 T | 6,000 A |
| 600 E | 4,000 I | 15,000 O | 40,000 M | 60,000 H |

. . . .

11. 677 × 209	12. 335 × 407	13. 683 × 279	14. 923 × 384

| 140,000 S | 120,000 L | 210,000 N | 360,000 T |
| 14,000 O | 160,000 T | 180,000 U | 3,600,000 M |

___ ___ ___ ___ ___ ___ ___ ___ ___
12   10   13   2   8   3   14   5   1

___ ___ ___ ___ ___ ___ ___ ___ ___ ___ ___
 9   7   2   13   7   4   5   14   11   6   13

Exponents

An exponent shows how many times a number, called a base, is used as a factor.

In 5^2, 2 is the exponent and 5 is the base. This expression is read "5 to the second power." It may also be read "5 squared." 5^2 means that 5 is used as a factor 2 times: $5 \times 5 = 25$.

In 2^3, 3 is the exponent and 2 is the base. This expression is read "2 to the third power." It may also be read "2 cubed." 2^3 means that 2 is used as a factor 3 times: $2 \times 2 \times 2 = 8$.

Here are more examples.

$3^2 = 3 \times 3 = 9$ $2^5 = 2 \times 2 \times 2 \times 2 \times 2 = 32$ $4^3 = 4 \times 4 \times 4 = 64$

$8^1 = 8$ Any base raised to the first power equals the base.

$6^0 = 1$ Any base raised to the zero power equals 1.

Caution: Be careful not to confuse an exponent with a factor.

8^2 does not equal 8×2 or 16. $8^2 = 8 \times 8 = 64$

Practice
Find each value.

1. 10^3 2. 6^2 3. 9^0 4. 3^4 5. 7^1

1.15 Horse Races

Horse racing is popular in the United States. The three biggest horse races in the country are the Kentucky Derby in Louisville, the Preakness Stakes in Baltimore, and the Belmont Stakes in New York. What are these three races known as?

To answer the question, match the number on the left with an equivalent number on the right. Write the letter that corresponds to each answer in the space above its problem number at the bottom of the page. One answer will be used twice. You will need to divide the letters into words.

1. 6^2 _____   N 256

2. 3^3 _____   W 49

3. 5^5 _____   O 27

4. 4^4 _____   L 729

5. 9^3 _____   P 512

6. 10^0 _____   T 3

7. 8^2 _____   I 36

8. 7^2 _____   E 1

9. 2^7 _____   C 64

10. 3^1 _____   R 128

11. 1^9 _____   H 3,125

12. 8^3 _____

___ ___ ___ ___ ___ ___ ___ ___ ___ ___ ___ ___ ___ ___
10   3   6   10   9   1   12   5   11   7   9   2   8   4

1.16 Review: Aerobic Exercise

Exercise is important for good health. Aerobic exercises are one kind of exercise. These exercises increase your heart rate, build endurance, and burn calories. There are many different kinds of aerobic exercises. What are three of the most common?

To answer the question, find the answer to each problem below. Match each answer to one of the answer choices in the list after the problems. Then write the letter that corresponds to each answer in the space above its problem number at the bottom of the page. Not all answers will be used. You will need to divide the letters into words.

1. Find the least common multiple of 6 and 4. _____

2. 5^2 = _____   3. 4^5 = _____   4. 3^4 = _____   5. 8^1 = _____

6. $\begin{array}{r} 95 \\ \times\ 30 \\ \hline \end{array}$
7. $\begin{array}{r} 548 \\ \times\ 700 \\ \hline \end{array}$
8. $\begin{array}{r} 85 \\ \times\ 46 \\ \hline \end{array}$
9. $\begin{array}{r} 289 \\ \times\ 65 \\ \hline \end{array}$
10. $\begin{array}{r} 827 \\ \times\ 74 \\ \hline \end{array}$

11. $\begin{array}{r} 405 \\ \times\ 378 \\ \hline \end{array}$
12. $\begin{array}{r} 684 \\ \times\ 543 \\ \hline \end{array}$
13. $\begin{array}{r} 5,389 \\ \times\ 267 \\ \hline \end{array}$
14. $\begin{array}{r} 6,805 \\ \times\ 3,582 \\ \hline \end{array}$

Answer Choices

153,090 **M**   25 **Y**   3,910 **L**   25,375,510 **F**   2,850 **S**
12 **A**   383,600 **U**   1,024 **G**   371,412 **C**   81 **I**   20 **T**
1,438,863 **B**   61,198 **R**   8 **D**   18,885 **H**   24,375,510 **N**
18,785 **W**   370,402 **X**

___ ___ ___ ___ ___ ___ ___ ___ ___ ___ ___ ___ ___ ___ ___ ___
10 7 14 14 4 14 3 13 4 12 2 12 8 4 14 3

___ ___ ___ ___ ___ ___ ___ ___ ___ ___ ___ ___
1 14 5 6 9 4 11 11 4 14 3

Dividing Whole Numbers

Division is an operation in which a quantity is divided (separated) into groups. The quantity, or number, being divided is called the dividend. The number that divides the dividend is called the divisor. The number, not including any remainder, that results from dividing is called the quotient. The remainder is the amount left over when a number cannot be divided evenly. Division is the inverse, or opposite, operation of multiplication.

Basic Division Facts

Because division and multiplication are inverse operations, you can use your understanding of basic multiplication facts to learn basic division facts.

$3 \times 4 = 12$	$12 \div 4 = 3$	$12 \div 3 = 4$
$5 \times 2 = 10$	$10 \div 5 = 2$	$10 \div 2 = 5$
$6 \times 3 = 18$	$18 \div 6 = 3$	$18 \div 3 = 6$
$2 \times 8 = 16$	$16 \div 2 = 8$	$16 \div 8 = 2$
$7 \times 6 = 42$	$42 \div 7 = 6$	$42 \div 6 = 7$

The division problem $12 \div 3 = 4$ can also be written like the example below.

$$3\overline{)12} \;\; ^4$$

In this example, 3 is the divisor, 12 is the dividend, and 4 is the quotient.

You can check that your answer to a division problem is correct by multiplying the quotient by the divisor. The product should equal the dividend.

$$3\overline{)12} \;\; ^4 \qquad 4 \times 3 = 12$$

Here are more examples.

$$5\overline{)25}\;\;^5 \qquad 6\overline{)24}\;\;^4 \qquad 3\overline{)27}\;\;^9 \qquad 8\overline{)56}\;\;^7 \qquad 7\overline{)49}\;\;^7$$

Practice
Find the quotients.

1. $6\overline{)54}$ 2. $8\overline{)24}$ 3. $4\overline{)32}$ 4. $9\overline{)72}$ 5. $7\overline{)21}$

Dividing Whole Numbers

2.1 The Kingdoms of Life

There are five kingdoms of life on Earth. One is fungi, which includes molds, mushrooms, and yeast. Another is protista, which includes amoebas, paramecia, and some algae. A third is monera, which includes one-celled bacteria that do not have a nucleus. What are the other two kingdoms?

To answer the question, find the quotients. Match each answer to one of the answer choices in the list after the problems. Then write the letter that corresponds to each answer in the space above its problem number at the bottom of the page. Some answers will be used more than once. One answer will not be used. One letter is provided. You will need to divide the letters into words.

1. $7\overline{)35}$　　2. $8\overline{)64}$　　3. $3\overline{)24}$　　4. $3\overline{)21}$　　5. $6\overline{)54}$

6. $6\overline{)12}$　　7. $8\overline{)72}$　　8. $8\overline{)40}$　　9. $4\overline{)36}$　　10. $6\overline{)36}$

11. $9\overline{)81}$　　12. $6\overline{)18}$　　13. $6\overline{)24}$　　14. $9\overline{)9}$　　15. $7\overline{)28}$

Answer Choices

8 S	3 I	2 M	6 T	5 N	1 P	9 A	4 L
7 D	0 R						

___ ___ ___ ___ ___ ___ ___ ___ ___ ___N ___ ___ ___ ___ ___
14 13 5   8 10   3   7   1   4   9   12   6 11 15   2

Factors, Common Factors, and Greatest Common Factors

A factor is a number multiplied by another number to find a product.

$3 \times 5 = 15$ 3 and 5 are factors of 15.

Since division is the inverse, or opposite, operation of multiplication, 3 and 5 are also divisors of 15.

$15 \div 3 = 5$ $15 \div 5 = 3$

To be a factor, a divisor must divide a dividend evenly without a remainder. Since 4 does not divide 15 evenly, 4 is not a factor of 15.

A number may have several factors. Following are some examples.

Factors of 2: 1, 2
Factors of 3: 1, 3
Factors of 8: 1, 2, 4, 8
Factors of 12: 1, 2, 3, 4, 6, 12
Factors of 20: 1, 2, 4, 5, 10, 20
Factors of 25: 1, 5, 25
Factors of 32: 1, 2, 4, 8, 16, 32

When a number is a factor of two or more numbers, it is called a common factor.

Factors of 18: 1, 2, 3, 6, 9, 18
Factors of 24: 1, 2, 3, 4, 6, 8, 12, 24

The common factors of 18 and 24 are 1, 2, 3, 6.

The greatest common factor (GCF) is the largest factor common to two or more numbers. The GCF of 18 and 24 is 6.

Practice

Find the factors and greatest common factor of each pair of numbers.

1. 4 and 10   2. 9 and 36   3. 14 and 30   4. 16 and 28   5. 21 and 27

2.2 Water and Energy

Water pressure can be used to turn turbines that generate electricity. What is this form of energy called?

To answer the question, read each statement below. If the statement is correct, write the letter for **correct** in the space above its number at the bottom of the page. If the statement is incorrect, write the letter for **incorrect**.

1. The only factors of 22 are 1 and 11.
   U. correct   **O.** incorrect

2. The greatest common factor of 54 and 45 is 9.
   O. correct   **E.** incorrect

3. The only common factors of 24 and 36 are 1, 3, 6, and 8.
   E. correct   **R.** incorrect

4. The greatest common factor of 21 and 28 is 14.
   G. correct   **E.** incorrect

5. All of the factors of 30 are 1, 2, 3, 10, 15, and 30.
   T. correct   **D.** incorrect

6. The greatest common factor of 14 and 16 is 2.
   W. correct   **R.** incorrect

7. The greatest common factor of 6 and 20 is 2.
   Y. correct   **A.** incorrect

8. The only common factors of 15 and 25 are 1, 3, and 5.
   N. correct   **R.** incorrect

9. All of the factors of 50 are 1, 2, 5, 10, 25, and 50.
   H. correct   **W.** incorrect

10. All of the factors of 42 are 1, 2, 3, 6, 7, 14, 21, and 42.
    P. correct   **N.** incorrect

Dividing Whole Numbers

$$\overline{}\ \overline{}\ \overline{}\ \overline{}\ \overline{}\ \overline{}\ \overline{}\ \overline{}\ \overline{}\ \overline{}$$
  9   7   5   3   1   10   2   6   4   8

© Judith A. Muschla and Gary Robert Muschla

Prime Numbers, Composite Numbers, and Prime Factorization

Numbers that have only two factors, 1 and the number itself, are called prime numbers.

2 is a prime number because its only factors are 1 and 2.

3 is a prime number because its only factors are 1 and 3.

101 is a prime number because its only factors are 1 and 101.

Following is a list of the first 26 prime numbers.

2	3	5	7	11	13	17	19	23	29	31	37	41
43	47	53	59	61	67	71	73	79	83	89	97	101

Numbers greater than 1 that have more than two factors are called composite numbers. (The number 1 is neither prime nor composite.)

4 is a composite number because its factors are 1, 2, and 4.

6 is a composite number because its factors are 1, 2, 3, and 6.

39 is a composite number because its factors are 1, 3, 13, and 39.

Following is a list of the first 26 composite numbers.

4	6	8	9	10	12	14	15	16	18	20	21	22
24	25	26	27	28	30	32	33	34	35	36	38	39

Every even number, except 2, is composite, because 2 is a factor of every even number.

Every composite number can be factored as a product of prime numbers. This is called the prime factorization. Only prime numbers can be used in prime factorization.

The prime factorization of 6 is 2×3.

The prime factorization of 18 is $2 \times 3 \times 3$.

The prime factorization of 20 is $2 \times 2 \times 5$.

Practice

Give the prime factorization of each number below.

1. 15   2. 10   3. 25   4. 24   5. 30

Dividing Whole Numbers

2.3 Sailing to the End of the World

In 1433, Portuguese explorer Gil Eannes sailed past a place in western Africa that was thought to be the end of the world. What place was this?

To answer the question, read each statement below. If the statement is correct, write the letter for **correct** in the space above its number at the bottom of the page. If the statement is incorrect, write the letter for **incorrect**.

1. 13 is a composite number.
   U. correct   **A.** incorrect

2. The two prime factors of 21 are 3 and 7.
   O. correct   **E.** incorrect

3. The prime factorization of 16 is 2 × 2 × 2 × 2.
   O. correct   **I.** incorrect

4. The prime factorization of 45 is 3 × 3 × 5.
   E. correct   **A.** incorrect

5. 32 is a prime number.
   N. correct   **R.** incorrect

6. The prime factorization of 36 is 4 × 9.
   O. correct   **A.** incorrect

7. The prime factorization of 28 is 2 × 2 × 7.
   J. correct   **T.** incorrect

8. The prime factorization of 56 is 2 × 2 × 16.
   R. correct   **P.** incorrect

9. 91 is a prime number.
   P. correct   **C.** incorrect

10. 100 is a composite number.
    D. correct   **S.** incorrect

11. The prime factors of 12 are 2 and 6.
    R. correct   **B.** incorrect

__ __ __ __   __ __ __ __ __ __ __
9 6 8 4   11 2 7 1 10 3 5

Dividing Whole Numbers by One-Digit Divisors

Division is a process in which you break numbers into groups. The steps for division are as follows: divide, multiply, subtract, compare the difference with the divisor, and bring the next number down. The process is continued until there are no more numbers to bring down.

$$\begin{array}{r} 3 \\ 2\overline{)68} \\ \underline{6} \end{array}$$

Divide 6 tens by 2 ones to find 3 tens. Write 3 in the quotient in the tens place. Multiply 3 by 2 to find 6. Write 6 under the 6 tens in the dividend.

$$\begin{array}{r} 34 \\ 2\overline{)68} \\ \underline{6} \\ 8 \\ \underline{8} \\ 0 \end{array}$$

Subtract 6 from 6 to find 0. Compare to make sure the difference is less than the divisor. If the answer after subtracting is larger than the divisor, you must increase the quotient and redo the previous steps. (Note that the zero is omitted.) Bring down 8 ones. Divide 8 ones by 2 ones to find 4 ones. Write 4 in the quotient in the ones place. Multiply 4 by 2 to find 8. Subtract to find 0. Compare the difference with the divisor. Since there are no more numbers to bring down, the quotient is 34.

Here are more examples.

For the first example, divide 13 tens (which is 130) by 3 to find 4 tens. Write 4 in the quotient in the tens place. Continue the process of division. When there are no more numbers to bring down and a number is left over, it is called the remainder and it is written after the quotient. A remainder must always be less than the divisor.

$$\begin{array}{r} 45\ \text{R2} \\ 3\overline{)137} \\ \underline{12} \\ 17 \\ \underline{15} \\ 2 \end{array} \qquad \begin{array}{r} 567\ \text{R3} \\ 6\overline{)3,405} \\ \underline{30} \\ 40 \\ \underline{36} \\ 45 \\ \underline{42} \\ 3 \end{array} \qquad \begin{array}{r} 2,202 \\ 7\overline{)15,414} \\ \underline{14} \\ 14 \\ \underline{14} \\ 1 \\ \underline{0} \\ 14 \\ \underline{14} \\ 0 \end{array}$$

You can check your answer to a division problem by multiplying the quotient by the divisor and adding the remainder to the product. Your answer should equal the dividend.

Practice

Find the quotients.

1. $3\overline{)69}$ 2. $5\overline{)85}$ 3. $8\overline{)407}$ 4. $6\overline{)2,532}$ 5. $7\overline{)35,635}$

Dividing Whole Numbers

2.4 The Iditarod

The Iditarod takes place in Alaska every year. It covers more than 1,150 miles (1,917 km) through rugged country. What is the Iditarod?

To answer the question, find the quotients. Match each answer to one of the answer choices in the list after the problems. Then write the letter that corresponds to each answer in the space above its problem number at the bottom of the page. Some answers will be used more than once. Some answers will not be used. You will need to divide the letters into words.

1. $3\overline{)81}$ 2. $5\overline{)97}$ 3. $2\overline{)46}$ 4. $8\overline{)89}$ 5. $4\overline{)92}$

6. $4\overline{)236}$ 7. $9\overline{)758}$ 8. $2\overline{)422}$ 9. $8\overline{)732}$ 10. $5\overline{)405}$

11. $2\overline{)242}$ 12. $3\overline{)633}$ 13. $6\overline{)726}$ 14. $4\overline{)844}$ 15. $8\overline{)769}$

Answer Choices

211 **D**	84 R2 **O**	81 **L**	121 **G**	23 **E**	59 **R**
27 **S**	102 **B**	96 R1 **C**	23 R1 **T**	19 R2 **A**	11 R1 **I**
91 R4 **N**	94 R2 **W**				

___ ___ ___ ___ ___ ___ ___ ___ ___ ___ ___ ___ ___ ___
14　7　13　1　10　3　8　12　4　9　11　6　2　15　5

© Judith A. Muschla and Gary Robert Muschla

Dividing Whole Numbers

2.5 Biomes

The Earth's land masses are divided into six large regions called biomes. Each biome has its own environment, based on climate and geography. Three biomes are the tropical rainforest, the taiga, and the temperate forest. What are the other three?

To answer the question, find the quotients. Match each answer to one of the answer choices in the list after the problems. Then write the letter that corresponds to each answer in the space above its problem number at the bottom of the page. Some answers will be used more than once. Some answers will not be used. Some letters are provided.

1. $4\overline{)783}$ 2. $3\overline{)291}$ 3. $8\overline{)706}$ 4. $3\overline{)903}$ 5. $6\overline{)582}$

6. $4\overline{)3,761}$ 7. $6\overline{)1,806}$ 8. $8\overline{)7,521}$ 9. $3\overline{)1,500}$ 10. $9\overline{)7,852}$

11. $5\overline{)8,749}$ 12. $9\overline{)4,500}$ 13. $4\overline{)20,442}$ 14. $8\overline{)40,882}$ 15. $6\overline{)50,736}$

Answer Choices

1,749 R4 **L**	195 R3 **U**	88 R2 **E**	500 **D**	845 R3 **M**
940 R1 **R**	5,110 R2 **T**	8,456 **G**	872 R4 **N**	301 **S**
1,950 R3 **W**	97 **A**			

  __   **R**   __   __   **S**   __   **A**   __   __
  15   2   7   11   10   9

  __   __   __   **E**   __   __   __   __   **N**   **D**   __
  12   3   4   6   13   14   1   8   5

Dividing Whole Numbers by 10 or 100

When dividing by 10 and 100, you must pay close attention to placing digits in the quotient correctly.

$$\begin{array}{r} 30 \\ 10\overline{)300} \\ \underline{30} \\ \underline{0} \end{array}$$

Divide 3 hundreds by 10 to find 3 tens. (Hint: To estimate, think $3 \div 1 = 3$ because $3 \times 1 = 3$.) Write 3 in the quotient in the tens place. Multiply 3 by 10 to find 30. Write 30 under 30 in the dividend. Subtract 30 from 30 to find 0. (Note that this zero is omitted.) Compare your answer to your divisor. Bring down 0 ones from the dividend. Divide 0 by 10 to find 0. Write 0 in the quotient in the ones place. Since there are no more numbers to bring down, the quotient is 30.

$$\begin{array}{r} 64 \text{ R5} \\ 10\overline{)645} \\ \underline{60} \\ 45 \\ \underline{40} \\ 5 \end{array}$$

Divide 6 hundreds by 1 ten to find 6 tens. (Hint: To estimate, think $6 \div 1 = 6$ because $6 \times 1 = 6$.) Write 6 in the quotient in the tens place. Multiply 6 by 10 to find 60. Write 60 under 64 in the dividend. Subtract 60 from 64 to find 4. Compare your answer to your divisor. Bring down 5 and continue the process of division. Place the remainder after the quotient.

Here are examples of dividing by 100.

$$\begin{array}{r} 8 \text{ R67} \\ 100\overline{)867} \\ \underline{800} \\ 67 \end{array} \qquad \begin{array}{r} 74 \text{ R32} \\ 100\overline{)7,432} \\ \underline{700} \\ 432 \\ \underline{400} \\ 32 \end{array} \qquad \begin{array}{r} 634 \text{ R93} \\ 100\overline{)63,493} \\ \underline{600} \\ 349 \\ \underline{300} \\ 493 \\ \underline{400} \\ 93 \end{array}$$

Practice
Find the quotients.

1. $10\overline{)456}$ 2. $10\overline{)798}$ 3. $100\overline{)6,394}$ 4. $100\overline{)3,892}$ 5. $100\overline{)74,938}$

Dividing Whole Numbers

2.6 Global Warming

When fossil fuels are burned, they release greenhouse gases, such as carbon dioxide and methane. These gases help to trap the sun's heat in our atmosphere. This in turn raises the Earth's temperature. What is the term that refers to the total amount of greenhouse gases that are released because of your activities?

To answer the question, find the quotients. Match each answer to one of the answer choices below each problem. Then write the letter that corresponds to each answer in the space above its problem number at the bottom of the page. Some letters are provided. You will need to divide the letters into words.

1. $10\overline{)382}$ 2. $10\overline{)506}$ 3. $10\overline{)230}$ 4. $10\overline{)945}$ 5. $10\overline{)674}$

3 R82 **E**	50 R6 **O**	23 **T**	94 R5 **T**	60 R74 **U**
38 R2 **A**	500 R6 **H**	2 R30 **H**	940 R5 **M**	67 R4 **R**

6. $10\overline{)500}$ 7. $10\overline{)999}$ 8. $100\overline{)487}$ 9. $100\overline{)609}$ 10. $100\overline{)3,004}$

50 **N**	90 R9 **I**	4 R87 **O**	6 R9 **Y**	300 R4 **E**
500 **S**	99 R9 **N**	40 R87 **H**	600 R9 **T**	30 R4 **C**

11. $100\overline{)5,898}$ 12. $100\overline{)6,075}$ 13. $100\overline{)93,182}$ 14. $100\overline{)62,904}$

58 R98 **I**	607 R5 **N**	931 R82 **U**	629 R40 **M**
580 R98 **A**	60 R75 **B**	9,310 R82 **E**	629 R4 **P**

15. $100\overline{)59,986}$

590 R86 **I**
599 R86 **F**

___ ___ ___ R ___ ___ ___ ___ O ___
  9   2 13   10   1   5 12   7

___ O ___ ___ ___ R ___ ___ ___
 15   8   4 14   11   6   3

© Judith A. Muschla and Gary Robert Muschla

Dividing Whole Numbers by Multiples of 10 and 100

The process for dividing by multiples of 10 and 100 is similar to dividing by 10 and 100.

```
      54 R27
30)1,647
   150
   147
   120
    27
```

Divide 16 hundreds by 3 tens to find 5 tens. (Hint: To estimate, think $16 \div 3$ is about 5 because $3 \times 5 = 15$.) Write 5 in the quotient in the tens place. Multiply 5 by 30 to find 150. Write 150 under 164. Subtract 150 from 164 to find 14. Compare to make sure 14 is less than the divisor. Bring down 7 from the dividend. Divide 147 by 30 to find 4. (Hint: To estimate, think $14 \div 3$ is about 4 because $3 \times 4 = 12$.) Write 4 in the quotient in the ones place. Multiply 4 by 30 to find 120. Write 120 under 147. Subtract to find 27. Compare to make sure 27 is less than the divisor. Because there are no other numbers to bring down, 27 is the remainder.

```
      212 R16
20)4,256
   40
   25
   20
    56
    40
    16
```

Divide 42 hundreds by 2 tens to find 2 hundreds. (Hint: To estimate, think $4 \div 2 = 2$ because $2 \times 2 = 4$.) Write 2 in the quotient in the hundreds place. Multiply 2 by 20 to find 40. Write 40 under 42. Subtract and compare the difference to the divisor. Bring down the 5 and continue the process of division.

Here are more examples.

```
      46 R49              107 R408
50)2,349            600)64,608
   200                  600
   349                  460
   300                  000
    49                  4608
                        4200
                         408
```

For this step, 460 cannot be divided by 600. Place zero in the quotient and multiply to find 0. (These zeros can be omitted.) Bring down 8. Continue dividing.

Practice

Find the quotients.

1. $40)\overline{978}$ 2. $30)\overline{754}$ 3. $70)\overline{2,408}$ 4. $50)\overline{9,352}$ 5. $800)\overline{42,759}$

Dividing Whole Numbers

2.7 An Early Conservationist

John Muir was a conservationist who helped save wildlife and forests. In 1890, he helped establish this special place in California. What is this place?

To answer the question, find the quotients. Match each answer to one of the answer choices in the list after the problems. Then write the letter that corresponds to each answer in the space above its problem number at the bottom of the page. Some answers will be used more than once. One answer will not be used. Some letters are provided.

1. $40\overline{)733}$ 2. $20\overline{)804}$ 3. $30\overline{)648}$ 4. $50\overline{)941}$

5. $40\overline{)420}$ 6. $80\overline{)2,065}$ 7. $90\overline{)3,786}$ 8. $60\overline{)1,278}$

9. $300\overline{)6,259}$ 10. $800\overline{)8,020}$ 11. $500\overline{)7,248}$ 12. $700\overline{)30,926}$

13. $400\overline{)21,672}$ 14. $900\overline{)27,048}$ 15. $600\overline{)64,379}$

Answer Choices

14 R248 **L**	18 R13 **M**	20 R259 **T**	107 R179 **N**	304 R8 **U**
40 R4 **S**	54 R72 **P**	25 R65 **E**	21 R18 **I**	10 R20 **O**
30 R48 **Y**	44 R126 **R**	18 R41 **K**	42 R6 **A**	

```
___  ___  ___   E   ___  ___   T   ___
 14   10    2         1    8         6

___   A   ___  ___   N   ___      ___   A   ___  ___
 15        9    3    5    7  11     13        12   4
```

Dividing Whole Numbers

42

© Judith A. Muschla and Gary Robert Muschla

Dividing Whole Numbers by Two-Digit Divisors

Use basic multiplication facts and estimation to divide by two-digit divisors.

```
      54 R15
32)1,743
   160
   143
   128
    15
```

Estimate by rounding the dividend and divisor. 1,700 ÷ 30. (Hint: Think 17 ÷ 3 is about 5.) Because you are dividing 17 hundreds by 3 tens, write 5 in the quotient in the tens place. Multiply 5 by 32 to find 160. Write 160 under 174 and subtract to find 14. Compare to make sure 14 is less than the divisor. Bring down 3. Divide 143 by 32. (Hint: Think 14 ÷ 3 is about 4.) Write 4 in the quotient in the ones place. Multiply 4 by 32 to find 128. Write 128 under 143 and subtract to find 15. Compare to make sure 15 is less than the divisor. Since there are no other numbers to bring down, 15 is the remainder.

```
       6
58)4,267
   348
    78
```

Estimate by rounding the dividend and divisor. 4,000 ÷ 60. (Hint: Think 40 ÷ 6 is about 6.) Because you are dividing 40 hundreds by 6 tens, write 6 in the quotient in the tens place. Multiply 6 by 58 to find 348. Write 348 under 426 and subtract to find 78. Compare to make sure 78 is less than the divisor. But 78 is greater than the divisor. This means that your estimate was too low.

```
      73 R33
58)4,267
   406
   207
   174
    33
```

Instead of 6, write 7 in the quotient in the tens place. Multiply 7 by 58 to find 406. Subtract 406 from 426 to find 20. Compare to make sure 20 is less than the divisor. Bring down 7. Divide 207 by 58. (Hint: Think 20 ÷ 6 is about 3.) Write 3 in the ones place. Multiply 3 by 58 to find 174. Subtract 174 from 207 to find 33. Compare to make sure 33 is less than the divisor. 33 is the remainder.

Here are more examples.

```
      4 R19            78 R8             82 R60
21)103            64)5,000          79)6,538
   84                448               632
   19                520               218
                     512               158
                       8                60
```

Practice
Find the quotients.

1. 82)328   2. 25)165   3. 41)5,068   4. 37)1,883   5. 95)5,630

Dividing Whole Numbers

2.8 Food Groups

Many scientists divide the foods we eat into five main groups. Protein foods are one group. Vegetables are another. What are the other three?

To answer the question, find the quotients. Match each answer to one of the answer choices below each problem. Then write the letter that corresponds to each answer in the space above its problem number at the bottom of the page. Some letters are provided. You will need to divide the letters into words.

1. 48)605   2. 82)656   3. 41)630   4. 18)203   5. 27)136

| 13 R1 O | 8 R10 P | 15 R15 I | 16 R15 A | 5 R1 T |
| 12 R29 U | 8 S | 15 R25 E | 11 R5 Y | 50 R1 G |

6. 59)826   7. 19)608   8. 21)630   9. 48)367   10. 39)700

| 14 A | 32 I | 30 D | 60 R38 E | 17 R37 I |
| 14 R3 E | 31 R18 U | 3 B | 7 R31 R | 18 R15 S |

11. 56)5,264   12. 81)5,323   13. 19)2,128   14. 53)2,206   15. 63)5,670

| 88 R16 F | 66 R68 S | 110 R16 V | 41 R33 F | 90 N |
| 94 G | 65 R58 R | 112 R | 41 R39 N | 91 R25 L |

__ __ __ __ __ S __ __ __ __ __ __ __ A __ __ __
11 9 6 3 15   14 13 1 7 5 2 8   10 12 4

44

© Judith A. Muschla and Gary Robert Muschla

2.9 Famous Nephews

Donald Duck has three nephews. What are their names?

To answer the question, find the quotients. Match each answer to one of the answer choices in the list after the problems. Then write the letter that corresponds to each answer in the space above its problem number at the bottom of the page. Some answers will be used more than once. Some answers will not be used. Some letters are provided. You will need to divide the letters into words.

1. $42\overline{)663}$ 2. $30\overline{)930}$ 3. $28\overline{)894}$ 4. $82\overline{)984}$ 5. $65\overline{)736}$

6. $21\overline{)315}$ 7. $41\overline{)492}$ 8. $19\overline{)798}$ 9. $42\overline{)630}$ 10. $37\overline{)2,886}$

11. $84\overline{)1,261}$ 12. $54\overline{)1,832}$ 13. $75\overline{)4,839}$ 14. $74\overline{)5,772}$ 15. $60\overline{)1,860}$

Answer Choices

33 R50 **H**	64 R39 **O**	42 **L**	30 R9 **V**	31 R26 **W**
15 R33 **A**	78 **Y**	31 **D**	11 R21 **N**	12 **E**	121 R6 **B**
33 R40 **J**	15 R1 **I**	15 **U**		

___ ___ ___ ___ ___ E ___ E ___ ___ ___ ___ ___ ___ ___ ___
12   9   4   14   15   3   10   1   5   2   8   13   6   11   7

2.10 A Common Corner

The boundaries of four states share a common corner. One of these states is Colorado. What are the other three?

   To answer the question, find the quotients. Match each answer to one of the answer choices in the list after the problems. Then write the letter that corresponds to each answer in the space above its problem number at the bottom of the page. Some answers will not be used. You will need to divide the letters into words.

1. $27\overline{)864}$ 　　2. $81\overline{)495}$ 　　3. $86\overline{)516}$ 　　4. $76\overline{)608}$ 　　5. $50\overline{)985}$

6. $36\overline{)5,238}$ 　7. $52\overline{)2,513}$ 　8. $21\overline{)4,509}$ 　9. $65\overline{)1,487}$ 　10. $87\overline{)7,308}$

11. $52\overline{)1,100}$ 　12. $24\overline{)2,688}$ 　13. $88\overline{)7,064}$ 　14. $16\overline{)3,248}$ 　15. $28\overline{)7,430}$

Answer Choices

320 K	19 R35 O	265 R10 R	214 R15 M	112 C
6 R9 N	203 A	22 R57 U	84 X　　8 D	6 I
48 R17 Z	11 R2 J	21 R8 W	145 R18 T	190 R35 G
32 E	80 R24 H			

___ ___ ___ ___ ___ ___ ___ ___ ___ ___ ___ ___ ___ ___ ___
14　15　3　7　5　2　14　2　1　11　8　1　10　3　12　5

___ ___ ___ ___ ___ ___ ___
14　2　4　9　6　14　13

Dividing Whole Numbers by Two- and Three-Digit Divisors

Dividing by two- and three-digit divisors requires careful estimation and computation of basic facts.

```
        48
  29)14,238
     116
     263
     232
      31
```

Estimate by rounding the dividend and divisor. 14,000 ÷ 30. (Hint: Think 14 ÷ 3 is about 4.) Because you are dividing 14 thousands by 3 tens, write 4 in the quotient in the hundreds place. Multiply 4 by 29 to find 116. Write 116 under 142 and subtract to find 26. Compare to make sure 26 is less than the divisor. Bring down 3. Divide 263 by 29. (Hint: Think 26 ÷ 3 is about 8.) Write 8 in the quotient in the tens place. Multiply 8 by 29 to find 232. Write 232 under 263 and subtract to find 31. Compare to make sure 31 is less than your divisor. But 31 is larger than your divisor of 29. This means that your estimate was too low.

```
       490 R28
  29)14,238
     116
     263
     261
      28
```

Instead of 8, write 9 in the quotient in the tens place. Multiply 9 by 29 to find 261. Subtract 261 from 263 to find 2. Compare to make sure 2 is less than the divisor. Bring down 8. Because you cannot divide 28 by 29 and there are no other numbers to bring down, write 0 in the ones place. 28 is the remainder.

Here are more examples.

```
      614 R9              82 R200
 63)38,691          723)59,486
    378                 5784
     89                 1646
     63                 1446
    261                  200
    252
      9
```

For this example, estimate by rounding the dividend to 60,000 and the divisor to 700. (Hint: Think 60 ÷ 7 is about 8.) Because you are dividing 60 thousands by 7 hundreds, write 8 in the tens place. Continue the process of division.

Practice

Find the quotients.

1. 52)4,678   2. 39)8,754   3. 74)38,246   4. 67)29,047   5. 328)49,563

Dividing Whole Numbers

2.11 A Great Cartoonist

Walter Lanz created a famous cartoon character. What cartoon character was this?

To answer the question, find the quotients. Match each answer to one of the answer choices below each problem. Then write the letter that corresponds to each answer in the space above its problem number at the bottom of the page. You will need to divide the letters into words.

1. $53\overline{)1{,}832}$ 2. $27\overline{)6{,}124}$ 3. $81\overline{)4{,}872}$ 4. $63\overline{)5{,}670}$ 5. $24\overline{)5{,}400}$

| 34 R30 **O** | 228 R2 **E** | 60 R12 **E** | 90 **E** | 225 R4 **T** |
| 34 **A** | 226 R22 **O** | 600 R12 **I** | 88 R15 **A** | 225 **D** |

6. $82\overline{)7{,}872}$ 7. $67\overline{)9{,}380}$ 8. $93\overline{)8{,}336}$ 9. $74\overline{)10{,}526}$ 10. $36\overline{)10{,}476}$

| 96 **R** | 141 R10 **O** | 89 R49 **N** | 142 R18 **O** | 291 **P** |
| 95 R24 **N** | 140 **W** | 89 R59 **K** | 143 **A** | 286 R12 **M** |

11. $19\overline{)49{,}630}$ 12. $48\overline{)73{,}064}$ 13. $521\overline{)36{,}525}$ 14. $922\overline{)66{,}198}$ 15. $224\overline{)11{,}475}$

| 2,613 **O** | 1,522 R8 **C** | 70 R55 **W** | 718 R4 **H** | 51 R50 **R** |
| 2,612 R2 **Y** | 1,524 R12 **N** | 705 R10 **T** | 71 R736 **O** | 51 R51 **D** |

___ ___ ___ ___ ___ ___ ___ ___ ___ ___ ___ ___ ___ ___ ___
13 14 2 5 11 7 9 1 15 10 4 12 8 3 6

2.12 American Territories

Guam, American Samoa, and the US Virgin Islands are three territories of the United States. What are two other territories?

To answer the question, find the quotients. Match each answer to one of the answer choices in the list after the problems. Then write the letter that corresponds to each answer in the space above its problem number at the bottom of the page. Some answers will not be used. You will need to divide the letters into words.

1. $63\overline{)1,646}$ 2. $26\overline{)2,200}$ 3. $18\overline{)2,432}$ 4. $60\overline{)7,584}$ 5. $31\overline{)9,840}$

6. $50\overline{)2,307}$ 7. $75\overline{)5,784}$ 8. $44\overline{)23,561}$ 9. $32\overline{)10,647}$ 10. $81\overline{)40,798}$

11. $39\overline{)16,761}$ 12. $148\overline{)26,057}$ 13. $846\overline{)72,834}$

14. $732\overline{)90,641}$ 15. $629\overline{)39,900}$

Answer Choices

86 R78 **E**	63 R273 **A**	332 R23 **S**	130 R52 **J**	176 R9 **C**
26 R8 **D**	535 R21 **R**	126 R24 **U**	123 R605 **P**	84 R16 **M**
503 R55 **L**	45 R17 **W**	46 R7 **H**	613 R5 **G**	77 R9 **O**
317 R13 **N**	429 R30 **T**	135 R2 **I**		

___ ___ ___ ___ ___ ___ ___ ___ ___ ___ ___ ___ ___ ___ ___ ___ ___
11 6 13 5 7 8 11 6 13 8 5 2 15 8 3 15 5 15

___ ___ ___ ___ ___ ___ ___ ___ ___ ___
3 9 10 15 5 1 9 15 5 1

___ ___ ___ ___ ___ ___ ___ ___ ___ ___
14 4 13 8 11 7 8 3 12 7

2.13 Amendments

In 1791, the first 10 amendments were added to the Constitution. What are these amendments known as?

To answer the question, find the quotients. Match each answer to one of the answer choices in the list after the problems. Then write the letter that corresponds to each answer in the space above its problem number at the bottom of the page. Some answers will be used more than once. One answer will not be used. You will need to divide the letters into words.

1. $23\overline{)7,841}$ 2. $64\overline{)6,656}$ 3. $33\overline{)1,486}$ 4. $99\overline{)4,456}$ 5. $49\overline{)5,880}$

6. $24\overline{)10,800}$ 7. $98\overline{)11,760}$ 8. $76\overline{)30,630}$ 9. $48\overline{)21,600}$ 10. $37\overline{)15,889}$

11. $486\overline{)39,854}$ 12. $516\overline{)96,094}$ 13. $103\overline{)82,868}$

14. $972\overline{)79,706}$ 15. $609\overline{)74,007}$

Answer Choices

804 R56 **F**   186 R118 **G**   120 **L**   45 R1 **I**   340 R21 **O**
12 R10 **N**   450 **H**   429 R16 **R**   104 **S**   403 R2 **E**
121 R318 **B**   82 R2 **T**

___ ___ ___ ___ ___ ___ ___ ___ ___ ___ ___ ___ ___ ___ ___
14   6   8   15   4   7   5   1   13   10   3   12   9   11   2

Dividing Whole Numbers

2.14 Animals

Warm-blooded animals such as mammals and birds have constant body temperatures under normal conditions. The body temperature of cold-blooded animals depends on the temperature of their surroundings. What are three kinds of cold-blooded animals?

To answer the question, find the quotients. Match each answer to one of the answer choices in the list after the problems. Then write the letter that corresponds to each answer in the space above its problem number at the bottom of the page. One answer will not be used. You will need to divide the letters into words.

1. 38)86,410   2. 25)52,003   3. 89)12,308   4. 55)25,274   5. 67)81,036

6. 183)14,786   7. 258)35,693   8. 379)74,090   9. 706)98,247

10. 974)89,165   11. 632)458,309   12. 526)665,836

13. 309)118,599   14. 706)307,402

Answer Choices

725 R109 **A**	139 R113 **P**	2,080 R3 **N**	138 R89 **H**
2,273 R36 **T**	195 R185 **I**	138 R26 **S**	1,209 R33 **B**
80 R146 **L**	459 R29 **R**	1,265 R446 **E**	189 R206 **V**
435 R292 **D**	383 R252 **M**	91 R531 **F**	

___ ___ ___ ___ ___ ___ ___ ___ ___ ___ ___ ___ ___ ___
11 13 9 7 8 5 8 11 2 3 10 8 3 7

___ ___ ___ ___ ___ ___ ___ ___ ___ ___ ___
11 2 14 4 12 9 1 8 6 12 3

2.15 A Method of a Great Mathematician

An ancient Greek mathematician devised a way to find prime numbers. His method bears his name. What is this method called?

To answer the question, find the quotients. Match each answer to one of the answer choices in the list after the problems. Then write the letter that corresponds to each answer in the space above its problem number at the bottom of the page. One answer will not be used.

1. $93\overline{)63{,}798}$ 2. $85\overline{)50{,}291}$ 3. $68\overline{)94{,}038}$ 4. $74\overline{)60{,}006}$

5. $220\overline{)468{,}352}$ 6. $307\overline{)950{,}040}$ 7. $956\overline{)742{,}638}$ 8. $806\overline{)943{,}100}$

9. $725\overline{)903{,}014}$ 10. $185\overline{)190{,}163}$ 11. $852\overline{)516{,}792}$

Answer Choices

686 **V**	1,170 R80 **R**	1,027 R168 **T**	2,128 R192 **O**
1,245 R389 **F**	3,094 R182 **H**	2,194 R242 **M**	591 R56 **N**
776 R782 **S**	810 R66 **A**	606 R480 **E**	1,382 R62 **I**

<table>
<tr><td>___</td><td>___</td><td>___</td><td></td><td>___</td><td>___</td><td>___</td><td>___</td><td>___</td><td></td><td>___</td><td>___</td></tr>
<tr><td>10</td><td>6</td><td>11</td><td></td><td>7</td><td>3</td><td>11</td><td>1</td><td>11</td><td></td><td>5</td><td>9</td></tr>
</table>

<table>
<tr><td>___</td><td>___</td><td>___</td><td>___</td><td>___</td><td>___</td><td>___</td><td>___</td><td>___</td><td>___</td><td>___</td><td>___</td></tr>
<tr><td>11</td><td>8</td><td>4</td><td>10</td><td>5</td><td>7</td><td>10</td><td>6</td><td>11</td><td>2</td><td>11</td><td>7</td></tr>
</table>

Dividing Whole Numbers

Estimating Quotients

When you are able to estimate quotients, you can easily tell if a quotient is a reasonable answer.

Here is an example. Maria divided 3,960 by 42 and found the quotient to be 940 R12. But her answer is incorrect, because she placed the first number in the quotient in the hundreds place instead of the tens place. This left her with an extra space, where she put zero as a placeholder.

Incorrect		**Correct**
940 R12	3,960 is about 4,000 and 42 is about	94 R12
42)3,960	40. 4,000 ÷ 40 = 100. If Maria had	42)3,960
378	estimated, she would have seen that	378
180	a quotient of 940 is too big.	180
168		168
12		12

Follow these steps to estimate quotients:

1. Round the dividend.

2. Round the divisor.

3. Divide. In many cases after finding your estimates, you will be able to divide mentally.

Here are more examples.

78)795 795 is about 800. 78 is about 80.
     800 ÷ 80 = 10. The quotient should be close to 10.

33)57,035 57,035 is about 60,000. 33 is about 30.
     60,000 ÷ 30 = 2,000. The quotient should be close to 2,000.

Practice
Estimate the quotients.

1. 8)785 2. 72)658 3. 12)4,896 4. 54)19,200 5. 46)21,400

Dividing Whole Numbers

2.16 A Big Desert

1. $7\overline{)890}$ 2. $95\overline{)509}$ 3. $32\overline{)3,394}$ 4. $82\overline{)7,568}$

| 90 A | 5 A | 10 C | 100 R |
| 900 S | 50 E | 100 A | 1,000 U |

5. $63\overline{)6,146}$ 6. $97\overline{)9,364}$ 7. $36\overline{)56,348}$ 8. $17\overline{)14,316}$

| 100 A | 900 U | 15,000 N | 5,000 U |
| 1,000 E | 90 R | 1,500 H | 500 I |

9. $36\overline{)78,436}$ 10. $64\overline{)25,049}$ 11. $72\overline{)31,352}$ 12. $46\overline{)32,998}$

| 200 S | 500 C | 400 S | 6,000 T |
| 2,000 A | 5,000 R | 4,000 O | 600 F |

| ___ | ___ | ___ | ___ | ___ | ___ | ___ | ___ | ___ | ___ | ___ | ___ |
| 11 | 9 | 7 | 3 | 6 | 2 | 1 | 12 | 4 | 8 | 10 | 5 |

Dividing Whole Numbers

Divisibility Rules

Certain whole numbers can be divided by other numbers without any remainders. For example, 6 is divisible by 2 because 6 ÷ 2 = 3. Understanding the divisibility rules that follow is important for many operations in math.

A whole number is divisible by:

- 2 if its last digit is 2, 4, 6, 8, or 0. Example: 804 is divisible by 2 because the last digit, 4, is divisible by 2.

- 3 if the sum of its digits is divisible by 3. Example: 321 is divisible by 3 because 3 + 2 + 1 = 6 and 6 is divisible by 3.

- 4 if its last two digits are divisible by 4. Example: 624 is divisible by 4 because 24 is divisible by 4.

- 5 if its last digit is 0 or 5. Examples: 25 is divisible by 5 because it ends in 5, and 500 is divisible by 5 because it ends in 0.

- 6 if it is divisible by 2 and 3. Example: 18 is divisible by 6 because it is divisible by both 2 and 3.

- 7 if after dropping the ones digit, then subtracting 2 times the ones digit from the remaining number, the answer can be divided by 7. Example: 721. Drop 1 from 721 leaving 72. Multiply 1 by 2 to find 2. Subtract 2 from 72 to find 70. Because 70 is divisible by 7, 721 is also divisible by 7.

- 8 if the number formed by the last three digits of the number is divisible by 8. Example: 6,432 is divisible by 8 because 432 is divisible by 8.

- 9 if the sum of the digits is divisible by 9. Example: 5,643 is divisible by 9 because 5 + 6 + 4 + 3 = 18, which is divisible by 9.

- 10 if the number ends in 0. Example: 600 is divisible by 10 because the final digit is 0.

Dividing Whole Numbers

Practice
State if the number is divisible by the number in parentheses.

1. 874 (2)   2. 90 (5)   3. 755 (10)   4. 94 (6)   5. 7,032 (8)

2.17 Ancient Field of Study

This branch of science studies the remains of ancient plants and animals. What is this branch of science?

To answer the question, read each statement below. If the statement is correct, write the letter for **correct** in the space above its number at the bottom of the page. If the statement is incorrect, write the letter for **incorrect**. Some letters are provided.

1. All three of the numbers 380, 4,275, and 12 are divisible by 2.
   E. correct   **N.** incorrect

2. Any number ending in 0 or 5 is divisible by both 5 and 10.
   N. correct   **G.** incorrect

3. Of the numbers 72, 94, and 534, only 94 is not divisible by 6.
   A. correct   **R.** incorrect

4. All even numbers are divisible by 2.
   O. correct   **H.** incorrect

5. Both 7,021 and 1,428 are divisible by 7.
   O. correct   **U.** incorrect

6. Every number ending in 9 is divisible by 9.
   A. correct   **L.** incorrect

7. All three of the numbers 960, 224, and 48 are divisible by 4.
   T. correct   **E.** incorrect

8. Every number that is divisible by 4 is also divisible by 8.
   I. correct   **O.** incorrect

9. The number 8,406 is divisible by 2, 4, and 6.
   A. correct   **P.** incorrect

10. The number 2,100 is divisible by 2, 3, 4, 5, 7, and 10.
    L. correct   **H.** incorrect

___ ___ ___ E ___ ___ ___ ___ ___ ___ ___ Y
 9   3   10   5   1   7   4   6   8   2

Finding Averages of Whole Numbers

An average is the number found by dividing the sum of a set of numbers by the number of addends. (Addends are numbers that are added.) Another word for an average is the *mean*.

Find the average, or mean, of the set of numbers below.

72	Add the individual numbers (addends).
34	Divide the sum of the addends by the number of addends.
28	Because there are four addends, divide the sum by 4.
106	
240	

$$4\overline{)240} = 60$$ 60 is the average.

Here is another example.

Rachel's test scores in math during the last marking period were 82, 93, 100, 95, and 95. What is her test average?

82	
93	Find the sum of the addends.
100	Divide the sum, 465, by the number of addends, which is 5.
95	
95	
465	

$$5\overline{)465} = 93$$ Rachel's average is 93.

Practice
Find the average of the following sets of numbers.

1. 33, 45, 50, 32   2. 106, 120, 115, 88, 96   3. 200, 202, 196, 210

Dividing Whole Numbers

2.18 Founders of a Political Party

In 1792 two men founded the Democratic Party in the United States. One of these men was James Madison. Who was the other?

To answer the question, find the average of each set of numbers below. Match each answer to one of the answer choices in the list after the problems. Then write the letter that corresponds to each answer in the space above its problem number at the bottom of the page. Some answers will not be used. One letter is provided. You will need to divide the letters into words.

1. 78, 71, 81, 69, 84, 79

2. 74, 69, 83, 86, 93

3. 121, 140, 138, 111, 120

4. 12, 18, 14, 17, 14

5. 80, 80, 80, 80, 80, 80, 80, 80

6. 18, 9, 12, 6, 15

7. 74, 92, 85, 90, 65, 75, 51

8. 112, 73, 135, 160

9. 241, 203, 215, 313

10. 200, 150, 100, 170, 300, 250

Answer Choices

243 M	15 E	80 O	75 P	81 R	126 S	11 G
77 N	232 U	195 J	76 F	70 Y	12 H	120 T

__ __ __ __   A __ __ __ __ __ __ __ __ __ __
8 6 5 9   3 10 4 7 7 4 2 3 5 1

2.19 Review: Measuring Humidity

Humidity is the amount of moisture in the air. What instrument measures humidity?

To answer the question, solve the problems. Match each answer to one of the answer choices that follows each problem. Then write the letter that corresponds to each answer in the space above its problem number at the bottom of the page.

1. What is the greatest common factor of 18 and 24? _____
   8 **E**   6 **C**   2 **S**

2. Of 21, 29, and 32, which is a prime number?_____
   32 **R**   21 **B**   29 **T**

3. Of 8, 13, and 31, which is a composite number?_____
   13 **U**   8 **O**   31 **N**

4. 875 ÷ 5 = _____
   175 **R**   17 R5 **M**   165 **T**

5. 705 ÷ 9 = _____
   82 R7 **W**   70 R8 **H**   78 R3 **M**

6. 180 ÷ 60 = _____
   3 **S**   40 **E**   35 **N**

7. 1,212 ÷ 41 is about _____
   40 **A**   300 **S**   30 **E**

8. 1,891 ÷ 56 = _____
   33 R43 **P**   35 R56 **C**   315 R21 **R**

9. 740,054 ÷ 705 = _____
   1,142 R82 **M**   1,049 R509 **Y**   1,206 R75 **E**

10. Find the average of the following set of numbers: 82, 70, 101, 93, 85, 79. _____
    90 **S**   85 **H**   86 **N**

___ ___ ___ ___ ___ ___ ___ ___ ___ ___ ___ ___
 8   6   9   1   10   4   3   5   7   2   7   4

© Judith A. Muschla and Gary Robert Muschla

Dividing Whole Numbers

Multiplying Decimals

The decimal system is a numeral system based on multiples of 10. A decimal is a number written in standard notation and usually contains a decimal point. Examples of decimals include numbers such as 0.6, 3.1, 4.56, 21.035, and 5.0 (which is usually written simply as 5).

Decimals are multiplied just like whole numbers, with one exception: the decimal point must be accounted for.

Multiplying Whole Numbers and Decimals

Multiplying a whole number by a decimal is similar to multiplying whole numbers, except that you must place the decimal point correctly in the product.

26	Line up the numbers in columns.
× 0.8	Multiply as you would with whole numbers, 26 by 8 to find 208.
20.8	Because you are actually multiplying 26 by 8 tenths, there must be a digit in the tenths place in your answer. Start at the right of your product and count one place (tenths) to the left and write the decimal point.

0.37	Line up the numbers in columns and multiply as you would with whole numbers.
× 45	
185	Because you multiplied a whole number by hundredths, there must be a digit in the hundredths place in your answer. Start at
148	the right of the product and count two places (hundredths) to
16.65	the left and write the decimal point.

Here are more examples.

94	72	246	45.1	1.346
× 0.5	× 0.07	× 0.32	× 342	× 26
47.0 or 47	5.04	492	902	8076
		738	1804	2692
		78.72	1353	34.996
			15,424.2	

Practice
Find the products.

1. 0.7 × 9
2. 42 × 6.3
3. 104 × 0.82
4. 4.364 × 29
5. 407.1 × 56

3.1 Sunscreen

Sunscreen can protect you from the harmful rays of the sun. Sunscreen is rated with the initials SPF and a number, for example SPF 30. The higher the number, the more protection. What do the initials SPF stand for?

To answer the question, find the products. Match each answer to one of the answer choices in the list after the problems. Then write the letter that corresponds to each answer in the space above its problem number at the bottom of the page. Some answers will be used more than once. Some answers will not be used. Some letters are provided. You will need to divide the letters into words.

1.	58	2.	4.6	3.	16	4.	0.32	5.	0.96
	× 0.6		× 9		× 0.8		× 48		× 16

6.	0.53	7.	5.6	8.	0.41	9.	0.49	10.	2.8
	× 45		× 38		× 73		× 86		× 76

11.	9.4	12.	215	13.	114.1	14.	0.607	15.	815
	× 63		× 0.65		× 40		× 39		× 5.6

Answer Choices

34.8 I	42.14 E	592.2 R	22.75 M	15.36 N	23.673 F
212.8 T	139.75 S	23.85 U	12.8 A	29.93 C	
34.4 W	4,564 O	41.4 P			

__ __ __ __ R __ __ __ C __ __ O __
12 6 5 2   13 7 9   10 1   4

__ __ __ T __ __
14 3 8   15 11

3.2 Diameter of the Earth

The diameter of the Earth is an imaginary line that starts at one point on the surface and goes through the center of the planet to a point on the other side. About how big is the diameter of the Earth?

To answer the question, find the products. Match each answer to one of the answer choices in the list after the problems. Then write the letter that corresponds to each answer in the space above its problem number at the bottom of the page. One answer will not be used. You will need to divide the letters into words.

1. $\begin{array}{r} 0.48 \\ \times\ 29 \\ \hline \end{array}$
2. $\begin{array}{r} 3.6 \\ \times\ 65 \\ \hline \end{array}$
3. $\begin{array}{r} 0.76 \\ \times\ 84 \\ \hline \end{array}$
4. $\begin{array}{r} 56 \\ \times\ 7.4 \\ \hline \end{array}$
5. $\begin{array}{r} 83 \\ \times\ 0.49 \\ \hline \end{array}$

6. $\begin{array}{r} 36.4 \\ \times\ 18 \\ \hline \end{array}$
7. $\begin{array}{r} 691 \\ \times\ 0.44 \\ \hline \end{array}$
8. $\begin{array}{r} 3.83 \\ \times\ 53 \\ \hline \end{array}$
9. $\begin{array}{r} 390 \\ \times\ 0.29 \\ \hline \end{array}$
10. $\begin{array}{r} 71.5 \\ \times\ 46 \\ \hline \end{array}$

11. $\begin{array}{r} 9.602 \\ \times\ 37 \\ \hline \end{array}$
12. $\begin{array}{r} 20.65 \\ \times\ 48 \\ \hline \end{array}$
13. $\begin{array}{r} 456.3 \\ \times\ 54 \\ \hline \end{array}$
14. $\begin{array}{r} 4,007 \\ \times\ 6.8 \\ \hline \end{array}$

Answer Choices

234 **S**	113.1 **L**	355.274 **H**	202.99 **R**	63.84 **D**
304.04 **U**	40.67 **A**	27,247.6 **E**	414.4 **T**	24,640.2 **N**
13.92 **O**	212.29 **J**	655.2 **I**	3,289 **V**	991.2 **M**

___ ___ ___ ___ ___ ___ ___ ___ ___ ___ ___ ___ ___ ___ ___
 2 14 10 14 13   4 11   1   7   2   5 13   3 13   6 13 14

___ ___ ___ ___ ___ ___ ___ ___ ___ ___ ___ ___
11   7 13   3   8 14   3 12   6   9 14   2

Multiplying Decimals

Multiplying a Decimal by 10, 100, or 1,000

You can multiply a decimal by 10, 100, or 1,000 by multiplying one place at a time.

3.9	Line up the numbers in columns.
× 10	Multiply as you would with whole numbers, 39 by 10 to
39.0 or 39	find 390.

Because you are actually multiplying 10 by 3 and 9 tenths, there must be a digit in the tenths place in your answer. Start at the right of your product and count one place (tenths) to the left and write the decimal point. Notice that 39.0 is the same as 39.

Here is a shortcut.

- To multiply a decimal by 10, write the decimal. Add one zero and move the decimal point one place to the right.

3.9	Write the decimal. 3.9
× 10	Add one zero. 3.90
39.0 or 39	Move the decimal point one place to the right.

- To multiply a decimal by 100, write the decimal. Add two zeros and move the decimal point two places to the right.

3.9	Write the decimal. 3.9
× 100	Add two zeros. 3.900
390.0 or 390	Move the decimal point two places to the right.

- To multiply a decimal by 1,000, write the decimal. Add three zeros and move the decimal point three places to the right.

3.9	Write the decimal. 3.9
× 1,000	Add three zeros. 3.9000
3900.0 or 3,900	Move the decimal point three places to the right.

Follow this pattern when multiplying by 10,000, 100,000, 1,000,000, and so on.

Practice
Find the products. Use the shortcut.

1. 7.43	2. 4.2	3. 86.7	4. 6.021	5. 73.85
× 10	× 100	× 100	× 1,000	× 1,000

Multiplying Decimals

3.3 C. S. Lewis

C. S. Lewis wrote many books. Among his most famous was a series for children. What series is this?

To answer the question, determine if the product for each problem is correct. If the given product is correct, write the letter for **correct** in the space above its problem number at the bottom of the page. If the given product is incorrect, write the letter for **incorrect**. Some letters are provided. You will need to divide the letters into words.

1.	2.	3.	4.	5.
7.9	0.84	9.6	0.37	4.6
× 10	× 10	× 100	× 100	× 1,000
790	8.4	960	37	460
H. correct	I. correct	I. correct	E. correct	I. correct
L. incorrect	U. incorrect	E. incorrect	O. incorrect	R. incorrect

6.	7.	8.	9.	10.
58.2	3.04	62.35	0.974	7.66
× 100	× 1,000	× 10	× 100	× 1,000
5,820	304	6.235	97.4	7,660
S. correct	T. correct	U. correct	N. correct	N. correct
M. incorrect	R. incorrect	O. incorrect	W. incorrect	R. incorrect

11.	12.	13.	14.	15.
39.6	7.543	0.2061	7.9	21.04
× 1,000	× 10	× 100	× 100	× 1,000
3,960	75.43	2.061	0.79	21,040
M. correct	N. correct	E. correct	N. correct	C. correct
T. incorrect	S. incorrect	H. incorrect	A. incorrect	T. incorrect

```
__  __  __  __  H   __  O   __  __  C   __  E   __
11  13  4   15      5       9   2       1       6
```

```
__  F   __  A   __  __  __
8       10      7   12  3   14
```

© Judith A. Muschla and Gary Robert Muschla

Multiplying Two Decimals

When multiplying two decimals, you must account for the decimal points in both factors.

$\begin{array}{r} 2.7 \\ \times\ 0.4 \\ \hline 108 \end{array}$	Line up the numbers in columns. Multiply as you would multiply whole numbers to find 108.

$\begin{array}{r} 2.7 \\ \times\ 0.4 \\ \hline 1.08 \end{array}$	Because you are actually multiplying 2 and 7 tenths by 4 tenths, there must be a digit in the hundredths place in your answer. (Tenths times tenths equals hundredths just as 10 × 10 = 100.) Start at the right of your product, count two places to the left, and write the decimal point.

Another way to place the decimal point correctly is to count the total number of digits to the right of the decimal point in both factors. 2.7 has one digit to the right of the decimal point and 0.4 has one digit to the right of the decimal point for a total of two digits. Count two digits (or places) from the right of your product to the left and write the decimal point.

$\begin{array}{r} 0.045 \\ \times\ 0.53 \\ \hline 135 \\ 225 \\ \hline 2385 \end{array}$	Line up the numbers in columns. Multiply as you would multiply whole numbers.

$\begin{array}{r} 0.045 \\ \times\ 0.53 \\ \hline 135 \\ 225 \\ \hline 0.02385 \end{array}$	Because you are actually multiplying 45 thousandths by 53 hundredths, you must have a digit in the hundred-thousandths place in your answer. (Thousandths times hundredths equal hundred-thousandths, just like 1,000 × 100 = 100,000.) Start at the right of your product and count five places to the left and write the decimal point. Since there are only four digits in your product, you must include zero as a placeholder. Your answer is 0.02385.

Remember, to place the decimal point correctly, you can simply count the total number of digits to the right of the decimal point in both factors. The decimal 0.045 has three digits to the right of the decimal point and 0.53 has two digits to the right of the decimal point for a total of five digits. Count five digits (or places) from the right of your product to the left and write the decimal point. Include any placeholders, if necessary.

Practice
Find the products.

1.	2.	3.	4.	5.
$\begin{array}{r} 85.3 \\ \times\ 0.06 \end{array}$	$\begin{array}{r} 0.062 \\ \times\ 0.07 \end{array}$	$\begin{array}{r} 2.5 \\ \times\ 0.34 \end{array}$	$\begin{array}{r} 7.02 \\ \times\ 3.1 \end{array}$	$\begin{array}{r} 34.67 \\ \times\ 0.293 \end{array}$

Multiplying Decimals

3.4 Daisy Duck's Nieces

Daisy Duck has three nieces. What are their names?

To answer the question, decide if the decimal point in the products below is placed correctly. If the decimal point is placed correctly, write the letter for **correct** in the space above its problem number at the bottom of the page. If the decimal point is not placed correctly, write the letter for **incorrect**. You will need to divide the letters into words.

1. $6.91 \times 0.49 = 3.3859$
   A. correct
   U. incorrect

2. $3.5 \times 0.07 = 0.245$
   I. correct
   Y. incorrect

3. $0.73 \times 0.41 = 2.993$
   Y. correct
   E. incorrect

4. $41.3 \times 0.6 = 24.78$
   L. correct
   M. incorrect

5. $9.6 \times 0.003 = 0.288$
   E. correct
   U. incorrect

6. $0.032 \times 6.1 = 0.01952$
   A. correct
   M. incorrect

7. $35.8 \times 4.3 = 153.94$
   J. correct
   R. incorrect

8. $3.04 \times 4.8 = 1.4592$
   U. correct
   P. incorrect

9. $0.538 \times 0.4 = 0.2152$
   N. correct
   S. incorrect

10. $0.005 \times 0.023 = 0.000115$
    Y. correct
    E. incorrect

11. $3.5 \times 2.61 = 0.9135$
    S. correct
    A. incorrect

12. $46.08 \times 0.34 = 156.672$
    E. correct
    R. incorrect

___ ___ ___ ___ ___ ___ ___ ___ ___ ___ ___ ___
11 8 12 2 4 6 1 10 7 5 9 3

3.5 Popcorn

This man introduced microwave popcorn to the world. Who was he?

To answer the question, find the products. Match each answer to one of the answer choices in the list after the problems. Then write the letter that corresponds to each answer in the space above its problem number at the bottom of the page. Some answers will be used more than once. Some answers will not be used. Some letters are provided.

1.	0.43 × 0.6	2.	3.2 × 0.9	3.	19.8 × 0.007	4.	9.02 × 0.06	5.	0.348 × 0.41

6.	4.51 × 0.12	7.	0.174 × 0.82	8.	70.5 × 0.65	9.	0.691 × 0.94	10.	2.35 × 0.54

11.	72.6 × 0.58	12.	0.342 × 0.68	13.	39.6 × 4.27	14.	0.398 × 25.1	15.	36.3 × 1.16

Answer Choices

2.88 **D**	0.64954 **N**	42.108 **L**	0.23256 **O**	1.385 **T**
0.5412 **E**	45.825 **A**	9.9898 **B**	0.1386 **C**	1.269 **H**
0.258 **I**	1.386 **G**	169.092 **V**	0.14268 **R**	67.81 **M**

```
___  ___  ___  ___  ___  ___  _E_
12    5    13    1    11   15

_R_  ___       _E_  ___  ___  ___  ___  ___  ___
 4    2             9    14    8    3    10   6    7
```

Multiplying Decimals

3.6 Fudge

Judy Blume has written many books for children. One of her most memorable characters is nicknamed Fudge. What is Fudge's real name?

To answer the question, find the products. Match each answer to one of the answer choices in the list after the problems. Then write the letter that corresponds to each answer in the space above its problem number at the bottom of the page. Some answers will be used more than once. One answer will not be used. Some letters are provided.

1.	3.8	2.	7.05	3.	0.045	4.	0.98	5.	1.9
	× 0.9		× 0.8		× 8.6		× 0.64		× 1.8

6.	6.8	7.	9.7	8.	1.96	9.	1.68	10.	62.9
	× 0.84		× 0.65		× 0.32		× 3.4		× 0.007

11.	5.08	12.	43.2	13.	7.06	14.	0.312	15.	0.936
	× 3.6		× 0.75		× 6.4		× 44.1		× 14.7

Answer Choices

32.4 T	5.712 R	13.7592 H	0.6272 L	45.184 Y
3.42 E	0.387 A	0.4403 X	7.315 N	5.64 C
18.288 F	6.305 D			

$\underline{\hphantom{X}}$ $\underline{\text{A}}$ $\underline{\hphantom{X}}$ $\underline{\hphantom{X}}$ $\underline{\hphantom{X}}$ $\underline{\hphantom{X}}$ $\underline{\hphantom{X}}$ $\underline{\text{R}}$ $\underline{\hphantom{X}}$ $\underline{\hphantom{X}}$ $\underline{\text{E}}$ $\underline{\hphantom{X}}$

11   6   8   5   13   7   1   10   4

$\underline{\hphantom{X}}$ $\underline{\hphantom{X}}$ $\underline{\hphantom{X}}$ $\underline{\hphantom{X}}$ $\underline{\hphantom{X}}$ $\underline{\text{E}}$ $\underline{\hphantom{X}}$

14   3   12   2   15   9

3.7 Peter Pan's Friends

In *Peter Pan*, Peter was a special friend of these three children. Who were they?

To answer the question, find the products. Match each answer to one of the answer choices in the list after the problems. Then write the letter that corresponds to each answer in the space above its problem number at the bottom of the page. Some answers will be used more than once. Some answers will not be used. One letter is provided. You will need to divide the letters into words.

1.	0.83	2.	3.1	3.	6.8	4.	9.6	5.	0.85
	× 0.07		× 0.8		× 0.27		× 0.45		× 7.9

6.	0.039	7.	0.34	8.	0.067	9.	2.43	10.	92.6
	× 8.6		× 5.4		× 0.008		× 0.99		× 0.009

11.	59.7	12.	7.29	13.	20.64	14.	57.31	15.	0.0348
	× 0.034		× 0.33		× 0.76		× 1.06		× 95.2

Answer Choices

0.000536 D	2.48 O	0.3354 C	2.0298 W	1.836 E
3.31296 I	0.8334 L	0.0581 H	0.332296 R	15.6864 A
6.715 J	2.4057 N	18.360 T	60.7486 Y	4.32 M

__ __ __ __ __ __ __ H __ __ __ __ __ __ __ __
11 7 12 8 14 5 2   9 4 15 6 1 13 3 10

3.8 A Great Purchase

In 1803, the United States purchased a large area of land from the French. What was this land called?

To answer the question, find the products. Match each answer to one of the answer choices in the list after the problems. Then write the letter that corresponds to each answer in the space above its problem number at the bottom of the page. Some answers will be used more than once. Some answers will not be used. Some letters are provided. You will need to divide the letters into words.

1. 8.52
    × 0.08

2. 6.04
    × 0.009

3. 0.0058
    × 0.7

4. 57.1
    × 3.8

5. 2.84
    × 0.24

6. 74.8
    × 4.7

7. 3.75
    × 0.73

8. 2.64
    × 0.69

9. 0.852
    × 0.094

10. 79.2
    × 0.023

11. 5.34
    × 6.02

12. 3.69
    × 0.214

13. 79.1
    × 0.648

14. 0.426
    × 0.188

15. 40.36
    × 7.02

Answer Choices

0.080088 T	206.88 M	0.05436 N	0.78966 L	2.7375 O
51.2568 Y	283.3272 A	351.56 H	0.00436 W	68.16 D
0.00406 E	32.1468 S	0.6816 I	216.98 U	1.8216 R

```
__  __  __  O   __  I   __  __  __  __  A
 9   6   3  12       4      11   1  15   2

     E   R           T
__  __  __  __  __  __  __
14       8   5       7  10  13
```

Multiplying Decimals

© Judith A. Muschla and Gary Robert Muschla

3.9 Thomas Edison

Thomas Edison is considered to be one of the greatest inventors of all time. What was his nickname?

To answer the question, find the products. Match each answer to one of the answer choices in the list after the problems. Then write the letter that corresponds to each answer in the space above its problem number at the bottom of the page. Some letters are provided. You will need to divide the letters into words.

1.	4.2	2.	0.63	3.	0.94	4.	2.07	5.	73.4
	× 0.8		× 0.5		× 0.68		× 4.5		× 0.87

6.	4.06	7.	2.78	8.	0.435	9.	8.021	10.	5.006
	× 3.9		× 0.49		× 0.32		× 5.6		× 0.034

11.	3.46	12.	42.8	13.	5.147	14.	42.06	15.	71.42
	× 0.084		× 0.79		× 0.37		× 0.0306		× 0.0059

Answer Choices

0.6392 **D**	0.170204 **R**	0.315 **I**	33.812 **H**	9.315 **T**
15.834 **N**	1.3622 **E**	0.1392 **O**	3.36 **M**	44.9176 **L**
0.421378 **W**	0.29064 **A**	1.287036 **P**	1.90439 **Z**	63.858 **K**

```
__  __  __  __  __  __   A   __  __  __   F
 4   12   7  15   2  13       10   3   8
```

```
__   E   __  __   O   __  __   R   __
 1       6   9       14  11        5
```

© Judith A. Muschla and Gary Robert Muschla

Multiplying Decimals

73

Estimating Decimal Products

. . . .

When you are able to estimate decimal products, you can easily tell if your answer to a multiplication problem containing decimals is reasonable.

Here is an example. Mariana multiplied 3.9 by 7.4 and found the product to be 288.6. But her answer was incorrect, because she did not write the decimal point in the proper place.

```
      3.9                    3.9
   × 7.4                   × 7.4
      156                    156
      273                    273
    288.6  ← Incorrect     28.86  ← Correct
```

Follow these rules to estimate decimal products.

1. Round each factor.

   3.9 can be rounded to 4.
   7.4 can be rounded to 7.

2. Multiply.

   $4 \times 7 = 28$

Based on this estimate, Mariana's answer was too large. The correct answer, 28.86, is close to 28.

Here are more examples with their actual answers and estimates.

```
   82.7 →    80         4.879 →      5         0.52 →     0.5
 × 0.94 →   × 1       ×   23.6 →   × 20       × 0.37 →   × 0.4
  77.738     80        115.1444    100        0.1924     0.20 or 0.2
```

Practice

Find the products first. Then estimate to see if your answers are reasonable.

```
1.   0.82     2.    33.4     3.    0.88     4.    75.1     5.  4,036.7
   × 4.8          × 0.78          × 0.81         × 34.3        ×  8.94
```

Multiplying Decimals

3.10 Adventure Tales

Among this noted author's works are *Kidnapped* and *Treasure Island*. Who was he?
  To answer the question, estimate the products. Match each answer to one of the answer choices below each problem. Then write the letter that corresponds to each answer in the space above its problem number at the bottom of the page. Some letters are provided. You will need to divide the letters into words.

1.	1.83	2.	4.59	3.	66.5	4.	6.74	5.	51.4
	× 2.4		× 6.3		× 9.7		× 8.25		× 65.9

40 **E**	30 **E**	700 **E**	560 **I**	35 **M**
4 **I**	0.3 **S**	70 **A**	56 **N**	3,500 **S**

6.	321.4	7.	7.4	8. 56.095	9.	9.66	10.	0.96
	× 62.8		× 1.8	× 40.5		× 19.4		× 3.45

1,800 **E**	14 **S**	2,400 **U**	20 **R**	3 **R**
18,000 **O**	1.4 **I**	2.4 **I**	200 **V**	30 **T**

11.	73.1	12. 10.746	13.	3.78	14. 0.9426	15.	0.21
	× 3.1	× 0.54		× 7.14	× 22.1		× 0.38

210 **L**	5 **T**	0.28 **O**	200 **E**	8 **A**
2.1 **S**	0.5 **N**	28 **B**	20 **O**	0.08 **R**

$$\frac{\quad}{10} \ \frac{\quad}{6} \ \frac{\quad}{13} \ \frac{\quad}{3} \ \frac{\quad}{15} \ \frac{T}{\ } \ \frac{\quad}{11} \ \frac{O}{\ } \ \frac{\quad}{8} \ \frac{\quad}{1} \ \frac{\quad}{5}$$

$$\frac{S}{\ } \ \frac{\quad}{12} \ \frac{\quad}{2} \ \frac{\quad}{9} \ \frac{E}{\ } \ \frac{\quad}{4} \ \frac{\quad}{7} \ \frac{N}{14}$$

Multiplying Decimals

75

3.11 Review: Missouri

The state of Missouri was named after the Missouri Indian tribe. What does the name Missouri mean?

To answer the question, find the products. Match each answer to one of the answer choices in the list after the problems. Then write the letter that corresponds to each answer in the space above its problem number at the bottom of the page. Some answers will be used more than once. Some answers will not be used. Some letters are provided. You will need to divide the letters into words.

1. $\begin{array}{r} 27 \\ \times\ 0.9 \\ \hline \end{array}$

2. $\begin{array}{r} 8.4 \\ \times\ 37 \\ \hline \end{array}$

3. $\begin{array}{r} 0.75 \\ \times\ 54 \\ \hline \end{array}$

4. $\begin{array}{r} 74 \\ \times\ 4.2 \\ \hline \end{array}$

5. $\begin{array}{r} 6.5 \\ \times\ 30 \\ \hline \end{array}$

6. $\begin{array}{r} 28 \\ \times\ 0.07 \\ \hline \end{array}$

7. $\begin{array}{r} 0.34 \\ \times\ 9.3 \\ \hline \end{array}$

8. $\begin{array}{r} 0.804 \\ \times\ 0.6 \\ \hline \end{array}$

9. $\begin{array}{r} 6.15 \\ \times\ 4.2 \\ \hline \end{array}$

10. $\begin{array}{r} 1.02 \\ \times\ 3.1 \\ \hline \end{array}$

11. $\begin{array}{r} 2.78 \\ \times\ 42 \\ \hline \end{array}$

12. $\begin{array}{r} 6.65 \\ \times\ 0.83 \\ \hline \end{array}$

13. $\begin{array}{r} 40.3 \\ \times\ 7.6 \\ \hline \end{array}$

14. $\begin{array}{r} 0.913 \\ \times\ 0.24 \\ \hline \end{array}$

15. Estimate the product: $9.7 \times 21.2 = $ _____

Answer Choices

0.4824 **G**	116.76 **S**	200 **L**	195 **R**	2.46 **M**
5.5195 **W**	24.3 **A**	0.21912 **C**	310.8 **E**	306.28 **F**
40.5 **N**	11.756 **P**	1.96 **T**	3.162 **O**	25.83 **H**

T __ __ __ O __ __ __ __
  7 12 3   13 6 9 2

__ A __ __ E __ __ N __ __ __
15   5 8   14 1   10 4 11

PART 4

Dividing Decimals

Except for needing to place the decimal point correctly, the process for dividing decimals is similar to the process for dividing whole numbers. You must divide, multiply, subtract, compare the difference with the divisor, and bring down the next number until the division process is completed.

Dividing a Decimal by a One-Digit Whole Number

You divide a decimal by a whole number the same way you divide whole numbers. The only difference is that you must place the decimal point in the quotient correctly.

```
      1.4
   4)5.6
      4
      16
      16
       0
```

Write the decimal point in the quotient directly above the decimal point in the dividend. Divide 5 by 4 to find 1. Write 1 in the quotient in the ones place. Multiply 1 by 4 to find 4 and write it under the 5. Subtract 4 from 5 to find 1. Compare to make sure 1 is less than the divisor. Continue the steps of the division process: multiply, subtract, compare, and bring down the next number until finished.

```
      0.07
   3)0.21
      21
       0
```

Write the decimal point in the quotient directly above the decimal point in the dividend. Divide 21 hundredths by 3 to find 7 hundredths. Write 7 in the hundredths place in the quotient. Write zeros as placeholders in the quotient in the ones place and in the tenths place. Continue the steps of the division process.

Here are more examples.

```
      7.6          5.1         0.0804         196.9          2.14
   6)45.6       5)25.5       8)0.6432      2)393.8        7)14.98
     42           25            64            2             14
     36            5            32           19              9
     36            5            32           18              7
      0            0             0           13             28
                                             12             28
                                             18              0
                                             18
                                              0
```

Practice
Find the quotients.

1. 4)9.2   2. 7)3.57   3. 5)0.845   4. 9)81.09   5. 8)0.06496

4.1 The Mouse

In 1970, this man received a patent for the "mouse" that is used with computers. Who is he?

To answer the question, find the quotients. Match each answer to one of the answer choices in the list after the problems. Then write the letter that corresponds to each answer in the space above its problem number at the bottom of the page. Some answers will be used more than once. Some answers will not be used. One letter is provided.

1. $4\overline{)23.6}$ 2. $5\overline{)23.5}$ 3. $6\overline{)0.846}$ 4. $8\overline{)47.2}$ 5. $4\overline{)4.96}$

6. $5\overline{)4.95}$ 7. $6\overline{)7.44}$ 8. $7\overline{)6.37}$ 9. $4\overline{)10.08}$ 10. $2\overline{)89.26}$

11. $8\overline{)5.032}$ 12. $6\overline{)267.78}$ 13. $5\overline{)4.7855}$ 14. $7\overline{)119.07}$ 15. $9\overline{)282.69}$

Answer Choices

0.141 **R**	2.52 **S**	1.034 **M**	0.99 **O**	0.9571 **N**
44.75 **I**	4.7 **U**	44.63 **A**	17.01 **G**	0.91 **T** 5.9 **E**
1.24 **L**	0.629 **D**	31.41 **B**		

```
__  __  __  __  __  __  __      __  __      G   __  __  __  __  __  __
11   6   2  14   5  10   9       4  13           7   1  15  12   3   8
```

4.2 An Important First

In 1929, Daniel Gerber made the first of this. What did Gerber make?

To answer the question, find the quotients. Match each answer to one of the answer choices in the list after the problems. Then write the letter that corresponds to each answer in the space above its problem number at the bottom of the page. Some answers will be used more than once. Some answers will not be used. Some letters are provided.

1. $6\overline{)4.44}$ 2. $2\overline{)5.04}$ 3. $4\overline{)75.6}$ 4. $3\overline{)0.243}$ 5. $7\overline{)7.28}$

6. $8\overline{)20.16}$ 7. $6\overline{)329.4}$ 8. $7\overline{)21.28}$ 9. $8\overline{)151.2}$ 10. $5\overline{)0.2035}$

11. $6\overline{)116.58}$ 12. $8\overline{)11.344}$ 13. $9\overline{)82.134}$ 14. $5\overline{)0.49035}$ 15. $4\overline{)2.1752}$

Answer Choices

0.0407 **R**	0.09807 **B**	0.74 **E**	1.418 **I**	54.9 **Y**	2.052 **L**
3.04 **T**	1.04 **D**	0.112 **M**	18.9 **N**	19.43 **C**	2.52 **A**
9.126 **O**	0.081 **S**	0.5438 **F**			

__ __ __ A __ N __ D __   __ __ B __   __ __ O __
4 8 10   12   1   14 6   7   15 13   5

__ I __ __   __   __ A __
   9   2   11   3

© Judith A. Muschla and Gary Robert Muschla

Dividing a Decimal by 10, 100, or 1,000

When dividing a decimal by 10, 100, or 1,000, you must place the digits and decimal point in the quotient correctly. Sometimes you may need to add zeros as placeholders.

$$\begin{array}{r} 0.04 \\ 100\overline{)4.53} \\ 400 \end{array}$$

Write the decimal point in the quotient directly above the decimal point in the dividend. Divide 4.53 by 100 to find 4 hundredths. (Hint: to estimate, think 45 ÷ 10 is about 4.) Write 4 in the quotient in the hundredths place. Write zeros as placeholders in the quotient in the ones place and the tenths place. Continue the process of division.

$$\begin{array}{r} 0.0453 \\ 100\overline{)4.5300} \\ 400 \\ 530 \\ 500 \\ 300 \\ 300 \\ 0 \end{array}$$

Because there is a remainder in this problem, continue by adding a zero in the thousandths place in the dividend. Bring zero down and continue the process of division. Add more zeros, if necessary, and continue until there is no remainder.

Here is a shortcut.

- To divide a decimal by 10, write the decimal. Move the decimal point to the left one place. Add zeros as placeholders if necessary.

  $2.7 \div 10 = 0.27$

- To divide a decimal by 100, write the decimal. Move the decimal point to the left two places. Add zeros as placeholders if necessary.

  $2.7 \div 100 = 0.027$

- To divide a decimal by 1,000, write the decimal. Move the decimal point to the left three places. Add zeros as placeholders if necessary.

  $2.7 \div 1,000 = 0.0027$

Follow this pattern when dividing by 10,000, 100,000, 1,000,000, and so on.

Practice
Find the quotients. Use the shortcut.

1. $4.2 \div 10$ 2. $3.14 \div 100$ 3. $86.5 \div 1,000$ 4. $300.2 \div 10$ 5. $5.187 \div 100$

4.3 New Citizens

In 1924, the members of this ethnic group officially became US citizens. What group was this?

To answer the question, find the quotients. Match each answer to one of the answer choices below each problem. Then write the letter that corresponds to each answer in the space above its problem number at the bottom of the page. You will need to divide the letters into words.

1. 0.4 ÷ 10	2. 37.2 ÷ 10	3. 5.1 ÷ 100	4. 0.25 ÷ 100
0.04 E	0.372 I	0.0051 O	0.025 A
40 U	3.72 A	0.051 I	0.0025 E

5. 6.13 ÷ 10	6. 22.36 ÷ 10	7. 0.4756 ÷ 10	8. 816.3 ÷ 100
0.613 A	2.236 S	0.04756 N	81.63 I
0.0613 N	223.6 N	4.756 A	8.163 T

9. 5.147 ÷ 100	10. 1.2 ÷ 1,000	11. 0.5 ÷ 100	12. 718.4 ÷ 1,000
0.05147 R	0.012 H	0.005 C	7.184 E
51.47 O	0.0012 A	0.05 M	0.7184 V

13. 62.08 ÷ 10	14. 9.58 ÷ 1,000	15. 40.03 ÷ 1,000
0.6208 C	0.00958 I	0.00043 A
6.208 N	0.000958 R	0.04003 M

___ ___ ___ ___ ___ ___ ___ ___ ___ ___ ___ ___ ___ ___ ___
13 10   8   3   12   4   5   15   1   9   14   11   2   7   6

Dividing a Decimal by a Two- or Three-Digit Whole Number

You divide decimals by whole numbers with two- or three-digit divisors the same way you divide whole numbers. The decimal point is placed in the quotient directly above the decimal point in the dividend.

```
      0.84
  42)35.28
     336
     168
     168
       0
```

Write the decimal point in the quotient directly above the decimal point in the dividend. Divide. (Hint: To estimate, think 35 ÷ 4 is about 8.) Write 8 in the quotient in the tenths place. Write zero in the quotient in the ones place. Continue the process of division.

```
        .
   52)3.9
```

Write the decimal point in the quotient directly above the decimal point in the dividend. Problems such as 3.9 divided by 52 cannot be completed without adding at least one zero in the dividend.

```
      0.075
  52)3.900
     364
     260
     260
       0
```

Add a zero as a placeholder in the dividend in the hundredths place. Divide. (Hint: To estimate, think 39 ÷ 5 is about 7.) Write 7 in the quotient in the hundredths place. Write zeros as placeholders in the quotient in the ones place and in the tenths place. Continue the process of division to find a remainder of 26. Because there is a remainder, add a zero in the thousandths place in the dividend. Bring the zero down. Continue the process of division until there is no remainder.

Here are more examples.

```
    0.13            2.16                                    0.032
 21)2.73         18)38.88         325)10.4      →      325)10.400
    21              36                                     975
    63              28                                     650
    63              18                                     650
     0             108                                       0
                   108
                     0
```

Practice
Find the quotients.

1. 54)102.6   2. 78)33.54   3. 26)19.5   4. 436)8.284   5. 604)809.36

4.4 Presidential Succession

The list of government officials next in line to become president should the president die, resign, or be removed from office is called presidential succession. After the vice president, who is next in line to become president?

To answer the question, find the quotients. Match each answer to one of the answer choices in the list after the problems. Then write the letter that corresponds to each answer in the space above its problem number at the bottom of the page. Some answers will be used more than once. One answer will not be used. Some letters are provided. You will need to divide the letters into words.

1. $12\overline{)4.32}$ 2. $70\overline{)25.9}$ 3. $33\overline{)0.594}$ 4. $18\overline{)6.48}$ 5. $24\overline{)8.64}$

6. $72\overline{)50.4}$ 7. $67\overline{)187.6}$ 8. $45\overline{)20.25}$ 9. $90\overline{)40.5}$ 10. $46\overline{)2.346}$

11. $96\overline{)100.8}$ 12. $36\overline{)777.6}$ 13. $92\overline{)4.692}$ 14. $108\overline{)339.12}$

15. $436\overline{)16.568}$

Answer Choices

3.14 **O**	0.051 **H**	1.05 **F**	2.8 **K**	0.36 **E**	105.5 **M**
0.018 **T**	21.6 **A**	0.37 **R**	0.7 **U**	0.45 **S**	0.038 **P**

__ __ __ __ __ __ __   O   __ __ E __ __ __ __ __
9 15 1 12 7 4 2   11 3 10   13 14 6 8 5

4.5 A Remaining Wilderness

This area is the largest subtropical wilderness in the United States. What is the name of this place?

To answer the question, find the quotients. Match each answer to one of the answer choices in the list after the problems. Then write the letter that corresponds to each answer in the space above its problem number at the bottom of the page. One answer will be used more than once. One answer will not be used. Some letters are provided. You will need to divide the letters into words.

1. $54\overline{)2.052}$ 2. $84\overline{)54.6}$ 3. $92\overline{)46.92}$ 4. $75\overline{)3.9}$ 5. $24\overline{)2.52}$

6. $29\overline{)19.14}$ 7. $52\overline{)43.68}$ 8. $90\overline{)9.72}$ 9. $74\overline{)3.774}$ 10. $96\overline{)499.2}$

11. $786\overline{)3,615.6}$ 12. $542\overline{)265.58}$ 13. $156\overline{)131.04}$

14. $302\overline{)1,630.8}$ 15. $654\overline{)2.4852}$

Answer Choices

0.105 G	5.4 T	5.04 Y	0.108 D	4.6 I	0.65 S
0.84 E	5.2 L	0.51 A	0.052 R	0.66 N	0.0038 V
0.051 P	0.038 O	0.49 K			

```
__  __  __  R   __  __  A   __  E   __
13  15   7      5   10      8      2

N   __  __  __  __  __      A   L   A   __  __
    3   14  11   1   6          9      4   12
```

Dividing a Decimal by a Decimal

When dividing a decimal by a decimal, you must first change the problem so that you are dividing by a whole number. You do this by multiplying both the divisor and the dividend by 10, 100, 1,000, and so on, depending on how many decimal places are in your divisor.

$0.6\overline{)1.92}$

$6\overline{)19.2}$

Because the divisor is 6 tenths, multiply the divisor by 10 to find 6. Multiply the dividend by 10 to find 19.2. (Hint: When multiplying a decimal by 10, move the decimal point one place to the right.)

$\begin{array}{r} 3.2 \\ 6\overline{)19.2} \\ \underline{18} \\ 12 \\ \underline{12} \\ 0 \end{array}$

Write the decimal point in the quotient directly above the decimal point in the dividend. Divide as you would divide a decimal by a whole number.

$0.85\overline{)0.3655}$

Because the divisor is 85 hundredths, multiply the divisor and the dividend by 100. (Hint: When multiplying a decimal by 100, move the decimal point two places to the right.)

$\begin{array}{r} 0.43 \\ 85\overline{)36.55} \\ \underline{340} \\ 255 \\ \underline{255} \\ 0 \end{array}$

Write the decimal point in the quotient directly above the decimal point in the dividend. Divide as you would divide a decimal by a whole number.

$0.007\overline{)0.0147}$

Because the divisor is 7 thousandths, multiply the divisor and the dividend by 1,000. (Hint: When multiplying a decimal by 1,000, move the decimal point three places to the right.)

$\begin{array}{r} 2.1 \\ 7\overline{)14.7} \\ \underline{14} \\ 7 \\ \underline{7} \\ 0 \end{array}$

Write the decimal point in the quotient directly above the decimal point in the dividend. Divide as you would divide a decimal by a whole number.

$0.42\overline{)84}$

Because the divisor is 42 hundredths, multiply the divisor and the dividend by 100. (Hint: The decimal point in both the divisor and the dividend is moved two places to the right. If you use this shortcut for this problem, remember to add two zeros as placeholders after the 4 in the dividend.)

$$\begin{array}{r} 200 \\ 42\overline{)8,400} \\ \underline{84} \\ 000 \end{array}$$

Divide 8,400 by 42 as you would divide whole numbers.

$$0.5\overline{)2.1}$$

Because the divisor is 5 tenths, multiply the divisor and the dividend by 10. (Hint: Move the decimal points one place to the right.)

$$\begin{array}{r} 4 \\ 5\overline{)21} \\ \underline{20} \\ 1 \end{array}$$

Divide 21 by 5. Because there is a remainder, add a decimal point and zero in the dividend.

$$\begin{array}{r} 4.2 \\ 5\overline{)21.0} \\ \underline{20} \\ 10 \\ \underline{10} \\ 0 \end{array}$$

Write a decimal point in the quotient directly above the decimal point in the dividend. Bring the zero down and continue dividing.

Practice
Find the quotients.

1. $0.6\overline{)2.88}$ 2. $0.08\overline{)0.528}$ 3. $0.46\overline{)2.162}$ 4. $5.6\overline{)15.344}$ 5. $3.45\overline{)4.14}$

4.6 Little League Baseball

The Little League World Series is held in the same town each year. What is the name of the town and in what state is it?

To answer the question, find the quotients. Match each answer to one of the answer choices in the list after the problems. Then write the letter that corresponds to each answer in the space above its problem number at the bottom of the page. One answer will be used more than once. Some letters are provided.

1. $0.02\overline{)0.464}$ 2. $0.6\overline{)0.36}$ 3. $0.5\overline{)0.77}$ 4. $0.03\overline{)0.261}$

5. $0.8\overline{)0.56}$ 6. $0.004\overline{)0.416}$ 7. $0.9\overline{)81}$ 8. $3.5\overline{)0.175}$

9. $4.8\overline{)3.36}$ 10. $0.75\overline{)24.75}$ 11. $0.24\overline{)1.128}$ 12. $3.6\overline{)151.2}$

13. $0.49\overline{)2.94}$ 14. $0.063\overline{)0.1512}$ 15. $9.6\overline{)69.12}$

Answer Choices

42 R	1.54 A	2.4 W	90 T	4.7 N	7.2 E	33 Y
23.2 S	0.7 I	0.05 L	8.7 M	0.6 O	6 P	104 V

__	I	__	L	__	A	__	__	P	__	__	__
14		8		5		4	1		2	12	7

__	__	N	__	S	__	L	__	A	N	__	__
13	15		11		10		6			9	3

4.7 A Presidential Slogan

This president was the first to use a campaign slogan. His slogan was "Tippecanoe and Tyler too," which referred to the Battle of Tippecanoe and his running mate, John Tyler. Who was this president?

To answer the question, find the quotients. Match each answer to one of the answer choices in the list after the problems. Then write the letter that corresponds to each answer in the space above its problem number at the bottom of the page. Some answers will be used more than once. Some answers will not be used. Some letters are provided. You will need to divide the letters into words.

1. $0.8\overline{)0.2}$ 2. $0.07\overline{)0.098}$ 3. $0.6\overline{)24}$ 4. $0.005\overline{)0.0025}$

5. $0.04\overline{)0.01}$ 6. $0.34\overline{)2.074}$ 7. $7.8\overline{)24.96}$ 8. $4.6\overline{)3.68}$

9. $3.9\overline{)12.48}$ 10. $0.88\overline{)0.4752}$ 11. $0.437\overline{)5.244}$ 12. $2.64\overline{)1.4256}$

13. $60.8\overline{)237.12}$ 14. $0.0345\overline{)0.1725}$ 15. $5.68\overline{)6.8728}$

Answer Choices

3.9 S	6.1 O	0.55 J	0.25 R	12 W	3.2 A	5 Y
1.4 M	0.54 I	0.5 H	0.8 L	0.061 T	1.21 E	40 N

__ __ L__ __ __ __ H__ N__ __
11 10   8 12 7 2   15   1 14

__ __ R__ I__ __ __
4   9   5   13 6 3

4.8 A Golfing First

Golf was played in Scotland as early as the 16th century. Who was the first notable woman golfer?

To answer the question, find the quotients. Match each answer to one of the answer choices in the list after the problems. Then write the letter that corresponds to each answer in the space above its problem number at the bottom of the page. Some answers will be used more than once. One answer will not be used. One letter is provided. You will need to divide the letters into words.

1. $0.004\overline{)0.024}$ 2. $0.5\overline{)0.525}$ 3. $0.08\overline{)0.1728}$ 4. $0.007\overline{)0.021}$

5. $0.6\overline{)0.0324}$ 6. $4.5\overline{)38.7}$ 7. $0.028\overline{)0.196}$ 8. $0.067\overline{)0.03551}$

9. $0.36\overline{)0.378}$ 10. $0.59\overline{)3.5518}$ 11. $13.5\overline{)116.1}$ 12. $50.8\overline{)314.96}$

13. $2.16\overline{)18.144}$ 14. $0.348\overline{)21.924}$ 15. $8.62\overline{)0.02155}$

Answer Choices

0.53 Y	8.4 Q	7.4 H	6.2 A	6 F	0.0025 C
3 R	6.02 E	2.16 N	0.054 U	7 T	1.05 O
8.6 S	63 M				

$$\underset{14}{\_\_}\,\underset{12}{\_\_}\,\underset{4}{\_\_}\,\underset{8}{\_\_}\,\underset{13}{\_\_}\,\underset{5}{\_\_}\,\underset{10}{\_\_}\quad\overset{E}{\underset{3}{\_\_}}\,\underset{9}{\_\_}\,\underset{1}{\_\_}\,\underset{6}{\_\_}\,\underset{15}{\_\_}\,\underset{2}{\_\_}\,\underset{7}{\_\_}\,\underset{11}{\_\_}$$

4.9 Illinois

The name for the state of Illinois comes from a French version of an Algonquian Indian word. What was the original meaning of this word?

To answer the question, find the quotients. Match each answer to one of the answer choices in the list after the problems. Then write the letter that corresponds to each answer in the space above its problem number at the bottom of the page. Some answers will be used more than once. Some answers will not be used. Some letters are provided. You will need to divide the letters into words.

1. $0.009\overline{)0.063}$ 2. $2.3\overline{)0.138}$ 3. $0.7\overline{)322}$ 4. $0.68\overline{)0.306}$

5. $2.7\overline{)0.0135}$ 6. $0.17\overline{)0.0765}$ 7. $0.035\overline{)0.315}$ 8. $0.92\overline{)0.0552}$

9. $8.4\overline{)0.2184}$ 10. $0.048\overline{)1.4976}$ 11. $62.3\overline{)336.42}$ 12. $3.09\overline{)26.265}$

13. $7.26\overline{)0.02904}$ 14. $50.4\overline{)1.3104}$ 15. $0.874\overline{)0.90896}$

Answer Choices

60.5 **H**	0.45 **I**	1.04 **M**	5.4 **O**	7 **F**	0.004 **T**
31.2 **B**	0.026 **E**	0.005 **P**	9 **N**	8.5 **S**	6.5 **L**
0.06 **R**	460 **U**				

__ __ __ __ _E_ __ __ __ __ __ __ _R_ __ _O_ __ __ __ __
13 8 6 10   11 1 12 3 5 9   4   2 15 14 7

Estimating Decimal Quotients

Many decimal quotients can be estimated easily. When you estimate decimal quotients, you can tell if the quotient is a reasonable answer.

Here is an example. Kristen divided 28.56 by 4.2 and found the quotient to be 0.68. But her answer was incorrect. She forgot to multiply the divisor and dividend by 10 so that she could divide by a whole number.

```
     0.68                              6.8
4.2)28.56  ← Incorrect    4.2)28.56 → 42)285.6  ← Correct
    252                                252
    336                                336
    336                                336
      0                                  0
```

Follow these rules to estimate decimal quotients.

1. Round the divisor and the dividend.

   28.56 can be rounded to 30.

   4.2 can be rounded to 4.

2. Divide.

   30 ÷ 4 is about 7.

Based on this estimate, Kristen's answer was too small. The correct answer, 6.8, is close to 7.

Here are more examples with their actual answers and estimates.

22.05 ÷ 0.9 = 24.5	416.52 ÷ 53.4 = 7.8	11.76 ÷ 2.8 = 4.2
20 ÷ 1 = 20	400 ÷ 50 = 8	12 ÷ 3 = 4

Practice

Find the quotients first. Then estimate to see if your answers are reasonable.

1. 1.7)5.78   2. 96.4)226.54   3. 0.9)67.5   4. 3.23)16.473   5. 12.2)21.96

4.10 Hometown for a Hero

Superman grew up in this town. What is the town's name and in what state is it?

To answer the question, estimate the quotients. Choose your answers from the answers below each problem. Write the letter of the more accurate estimate in the space above the problem's number at the bottom of the page. One letter is provided. You will need to divide the letters into words.

Dividing Decimals

1. 0.89)2.848   2. 4.2)25.2   3. 37.9)193.29   4. 0.9)5.67

0.3 E   6 A   5 A   6 L
3 I   60 W   6 R   0.6 O

5. 23.8)21.42   6. 30.5)183   7. 2.5)2.75   8. 0.85)0.935

10 U   6 M   10 N   10 R
1 A   60 E   1 S   1 L

9. 4.9)99.47   10. 78.4)161.12   11. 0.698)4.0484   12. 0.7)0.686

20 S   2 V   4 N   9 R
25 O   20 S   40 E   1 L

13. 4.76)17.8512   14. 1.25)25   15. 0.99)5.743

40 M   25 S   5 T
4 K   250 N   6 L

                                    E
___ ___ ___ ___ ___ ___ ___ ___ ___   ___ ___ ___ ___ ___ ___
14 6   2   15 12 10 1   8   4   13 3   11 9   5   7

93

Decimal Quotients That Repeat

Decimal quotients may be terminating or repeating. An example of a terminating decimal is 0.5. An example of a repeating decimal is 0.333. . . . The last digit, 3, keeps repeating without end. A bar may be written over a digit (or set of digits) to show that the digit repeats. 0.333 . . . = $0.\bar{3}$.

Sometimes decimal quotients repeat.

```
  0.2
9)2.2
  18
   4
```

Divide 2.2 by 9 to find 2 tenths. Multiply, subtract, and compare the difference with the divisor.

```
  0.244
9)2.200
  18
  40
  36
  40
  36
   4
```

Because there is a remainder, add a zero in the dividend in the hundredths place. Bring the zero down. Divide, multiply, subtract. Compare the difference with the divisor. Again, there is a remainder of 4. Add a zero in the dividend in the thousandths place. Bring the zero down. Divide, multiply, and subtract. Compare the difference with the divisor. Because it is now clear that this pattern will continue to repeat, write the quotient as $0.2\bar{4}$.

Here are more examples.

```
            3.366 = 3.3̄6̄                    20.9̄0̄9̄
0.3)1.01 → 3)10.100          1.1)23 → 11)230.000
            9                              22
            11                             100
             9                              99
            20                             100
            18                              99
            20                               1
            18
             2
```

Practice
Find the quotients.

1. 9)14.2   2. 6)5.6   3. 3)15.4   4. 1.5)26.5   5. 3.6)34.8

4.11 Words of a Cartoon Star

The cartoon character Snagglepuss had a favorite phrase that he would often say. What was this phrase?

To answer the question, find the quotients. The quotients may be terminating or repeating decimals. Match each answer to one of the answer choices in the list after the problems. Then write the letter that corresponds to each answer in the space above its problem number at the bottom of the page. Some answers will be used more than once. One answer will not be used. Some letters are provided. You will need to divide the letters into words.

1. $4\overline{)13.5}$ 2. $0.9\overline{)2.2}$ 3. $5\overline{)0.66}$ 4. $1.8\overline{)12.8}$ 5. $1.5\overline{)5.6}$

6. $5\overline{)11.81}$ 7. $1.5\overline{)0.093}$ 8. $3.6\overline{)25.6}$ 9. $2.5\overline{)47}$ 10. $0.78\overline{)6.5}$

11. $0.75\overline{)0.0465}$ 12. $1.2\overline{)15.8}$ 13. $6.6\overline{)15.6}$ 14. $0.56\overline{)1.176}$ 15. $8.4\overline{)35}$

Answer Choices

2.362 Y	2.1 H	$2.\overline{4}$ R	18.8 T	$2.\overline{36}$ G	$7.\overline{1}$ O
$3.7\overline{3}$ N	0.062 A	$8.\overline{3}$ V	3.375 S	$4.1\overline{6}$ M	0.244 F
0.132 E	$13.1\overline{6}$ D				

$\underline{}\ \underline{E}\ \underline{}\ \underline{}\ \underline{E}\ \underline{}\ \underline{}\ \underline{}\ \underline{}\ \underline{}\ \underline{R}\ \underline{}\ \underline{T}\ \underline{}\ \underline{}\ \underline{}\ \underline{}$

14　11　10　　5　1　9　4　15　3　　13　7　　2　8　6　12

4.12 Sneezing

When you sneeze, air is forced through your nose at a high rate of speed. About how fast is air forced through your nose when you sneeze?

To answer the question, find the quotients. The quotients may be terminating or repeating decimals. Match each answer to one of the answer choices in the list after the problems. Then write the letter that corresponds to each answer in the space above its problem number at the bottom of the page. Some answers will be used more than once. Some answers will not be used. Some letters are provided. You will need to divide the letters into words.

1. $0.9\overline{)5.1}$
2. $0.8\overline{)26.4}$
3. $3.6\overline{)0.198}$
4. $11\overline{)8}$
5. $3\overline{)1.1}$

6. $0.09\overline{)7.01}$
7. $6.6\overline{)2.1}$
8. $9\overline{)0.495}$
9. $0.44\overline{)38.5}$
10. $0.24\overline{)7.92}$

11. $0.27\overline{)3.333}$
12. $90\overline{)51.7}$
13. $0.88\overline{)77}$
14. $0.39\overline{)2.002}$
15. $8.25\overline{)5.75}$

Answer Choices

$0.3\overline{18}$ **S**	$0.57\overline{4}$ **L**	0.055 **R**	$0.30\overline{6}$ **T**	$77.\overline{8}$ **H**
$5.1\overline{3}$ **O**	$12.3\overline{4}$ **N**	0.5 **K**	$0.7\overline{2}$ **I**	33 **E** 87.5 **U**
$5.\overline{6}$ **M**	$0.3\overline{6}$ **D**	$0.\overline{69}$ **P**		

__	__	H	__	N	__	__	E	D	__	__	__	E	__
14	11	10	9	5	3		1	4	12				7

__	__	R	__	O	__	__
15	2	6	13	8		

4.13 Review: Emmy-Winning Cartoon

This cartoon show was the first to receive an Emmy for outstanding achievement in the field of children's programming. The show was named after its starring character. Who was he?

To answer the question, solve the problems. Match each answer to one of the answer choices that follow each problem. Then write the letter that corresponds to each answer in the space above its problem number at the bottom of the page. Some letters are provided. You will need to divide the letters into words.

1. $1.92 \div 0.6 =$ _____
   32 **U**   0.302 **S**   3.2 **Y**

2. $67.5 \div 5 =$ _____
   13.5 **C**   1.35 **L**   0.356 **O**

3. $0.2856 \div 0.008 =$ _____
   3.572 **E**   35.7 **N**   0.0357 **A**

4. $789.6 \div 4.8 =$ _____
   0.1644 **A**   1.64 **U**   164.5 **E**

5. $0.7544 \div 0.082 =$ _____
   0.0092 **R**   0.0925 **N**   9.2 **K**

6. $1.61 \div 3.5 =$ _____
   46 **P**   0.46 **B**   4.62 **S**

7. $17.787 \div 53.9 =$ _____
   0.33 **U**   3.337 **E**   3.03 **A**

8. $19.84 \div 5.2$ is about _____.
   4 **R**   3 **U**   6 **N**

9. $7.1 \div 0.9 =$ _____
   7.97 **E** $7.\overline{8}$ **D** $7.0\overline{8}$ **O**

10. $5 \div 6 =$ _____
    0.83 **F** $0.8\overline{3}$ **H**   1.2 **M**

__ __ __ __ L __ __ __ __ __ __ __ O __ __ __
10 7 2 5   4 6 4 8 8 1 10   7 3 9

Multiplying Fractions

A fraction is a number that names a part of a group or a part of a whole. A fraction has a numerator and a denominator. In the fraction $\frac{2}{3}$, 2 is the numerator and 3 is the denominator. The numerator, 2, shows how many parts of the group you have. The denominator, 3, shows that the group has a total of 3 parts.

Simplifying Fractions

A fraction is in simplest form when the numerator and denominator have no common factors greater than 1.

To simplify a fraction: Divide both the numerator and the denominator by their greatest common factor. (If you do not choose the greatest common factor the first time, choose another common factor and continue simplifying until the numerator and denominator have no common factors greater than 1.)

Simplify $\frac{6}{8}$.   The greatest common factor of 6 and 8 is 2.

$\frac{6 \div 2}{8 \div 2} = \frac{3}{4}$ Because 3 and 4 have no common factor greater than 1, the fraction is simplified.

Here are more examples.

$\frac{12}{18} = \frac{12 \div 6}{18 \div 6} = \frac{2}{3}$ $\frac{14}{35} = \frac{14 \div 7}{35 \div 7} = \frac{2}{5}$ $\frac{21}{24} = \frac{21 \div 3}{24 \div 3} = \frac{7}{8}$

A mixed number is a number made up of a whole-number part and a fraction part. An example of a mixed number is $9\frac{3}{5}$. The fraction part of many mixed numbers can be simplified.

$7\frac{8}{12} = 7\frac{2}{3}$ The greatest common factor of 8 and 12 is 4.

$21\frac{10}{15} = 21\frac{2}{3}$ The greatest common factor of 10 and 15 is 5.

$4\frac{22}{33} = 4\frac{2}{3}$ The greatest common factor of 22 and 33 is 11.

Practice
Simplify.

1. $\frac{8}{10}$ 2. $\frac{27}{30}$ 3. $\frac{6}{20}$ 4. $3\frac{9}{12}$ 5. $16\frac{35}{45}$

Multiplying Fractions

5.1 Garbage

On average, each American produces about 1,600 pounds (726 kg) of garbage every year. Where does most of the trash wind up?

To answer the question, simplify the fractions. Match each answer to one of the answer choices in the list after the problems. Then write the letter that corresponds to each answer in the space above its problem number at the bottom of the page. Some answers will be used more than once. Some letters are provided. You will need to divide the letters into words.

1. $\dfrac{8}{16}$

2. $3\dfrac{6}{8}$

3. $9\dfrac{10}{16}$

4. $\dfrac{24}{32}$

5. $\dfrac{8}{12}$

6. $\dfrac{4}{12}$

7. $3\dfrac{24}{32}$

8. $\dfrac{20}{24}$

9. $1\dfrac{9}{15}$

10. $\dfrac{9}{12}$

11. $\dfrac{6}{36}$

12. $\dfrac{18}{27}$

13. $4\dfrac{6}{16}$

14. $7\dfrac{8}{32}$

15. $\dfrac{16}{28}$

Answer Choices

$3\dfrac{3}{4}$ N $\dfrac{1}{6}$ A $\dfrac{2}{3}$ L $\dfrac{4}{7}$ F $\dfrac{1}{2}$ O $\dfrac{1}{3}$ T

$\dfrac{5}{6}$ D $9\dfrac{5}{8}$ E $4\dfrac{3}{8}$ R $1\dfrac{3}{5}$ S $\dfrac{3}{4}$ I $7\dfrac{1}{4}$ C

___ A ___ ___ ___ ___ L ___ S ___ N D
12   7 8 15 4   5   11

___ N ___ I ___ ___ R A ___ ___ ___ ___
10   14   2   3   6 1 13 9

Renaming Mixed Numbers as Improper Fractions and Improper Fractions as Mixed Numbers

Mixed numbers are numbers that have a whole-number part and a fraction part. $7\frac{9}{10}$ is an example of a mixed number.

An improper fraction is a fraction in which the numerator is equal to or greater than the denominator. $\frac{8}{3}$ and $\frac{4}{2}$ are examples of improper fractions. Improper fractions are usually changed to whole or mixed numbers and simplified.

Follow the steps below to rename a mixed number as an improper fraction.

Example: Rename $3\frac{4}{5}$ as an improper fraction.

1. Multiply the whole number by the denominator of the fraction. $5 \times 3 = 15$.

2. Add the numerator to the product. $15 + 4 = 19$.

3. Write the sum over the denominator. $\frac{19}{5}$ $3\frac{4}{5} = \frac{19}{5}$

Follow the steps below to rename an improper fraction as a mixed number.

Example: Rename $\frac{16}{6}$ as a mixed number.

1. Divide the numerator by the denominator. $16 \div 6 = 2$, remainder 4.

2. The quotient, 2, represents the whole number. The remainder, 4, represents the numerator of the fraction. The denominator stays the same. The mixed number is $2\frac{4}{6}$. Simplify, if necessary. $2\frac{4}{6} = 2\frac{2}{3}$

3. If there is no remainder, the improper fraction is written as a whole number. $\frac{15}{3} = 5$

Practice
Rename the mixed numbers as improper fractions and the improper fractions as mixed numbers.

1. $3\frac{3}{4}$ 2. $\frac{22}{7}$ 3. $4\frac{2}{5}$ 4. $\frac{18}{5}$ 5. $\frac{24}{3}$

5.2 Alphabets

An alphabet is a set of letters or symbols used to write the words of a language. Many languages, including modern English, are written in the Latin alphabet. What are three other major alphabets used around the world?

To answer the question, match the mixed or whole number on the left with its equivalent improper fraction on the right. Write the letter of each answer in the space above its problem number at the bottom of the page.

Mixed or Whole Number   **Improper Fraction**

1. $5\frac{2}{5}$ = _____   W $\frac{31}{2}$

2. $6\frac{2}{3}$ = _____   I $\frac{51}{8}$

3. 8 = _____   G $\frac{31}{4}$

4. $15\frac{1}{2}$ = _____   C $\frac{20}{3}$

5. $1\frac{2}{3}$ = _____   H $\frac{29}{8}$

6. $6\frac{3}{8}$ = _____   R $\frac{16}{2}$

7. $6\frac{3}{4}$ = _____   A $\frac{27}{5}$

8. $7\frac{3}{4}$ = _____   K $\frac{5}{3}$

9. $3\frac{5}{8}$ = _____   E $\frac{44}{5}$

10. $8\frac{4}{5}$ = _____   B $\frac{27}{4}$

___ ___ ___ ___ ___   ___ ___ ___ ___ ___ ___   ___ ___ ___ ___ ___ ___
 8   3 10 10   5   1   3   1   7   6   2   9 10   7   3 10   4

Multiplying Whole Numbers and Fractions

When you multiply a whole number by a fraction, you are multiplying the fraction by a number a specific number of times. For example, multiplying $2 \times \frac{1}{3}$ is the same as finding two groups of $\frac{1}{3}$. This can be shown as ■□□ ■□□, which can be written as $2 \times \frac{1}{3} = \frac{2}{3}$.

Here is another way to multiply $2 \times \frac{1}{3}$.

1. Write the whole number over 1. $\frac{2}{1}$

2. Write the problem. $\frac{2}{1} \times \frac{1}{3}$

3. Multiply the numerators and multiply the denominators to find your answer.

$$\frac{2}{1} \times \frac{1}{3} = \frac{2}{3}$$

Here are more examples. Remember to simplify, if necessary.

$$5 \times \frac{1}{6} = \frac{5}{1} \times \frac{1}{6} = \frac{5}{6}$$

$$7 \times \frac{3}{4} = \frac{7}{1} \times \frac{3}{4} = \frac{21}{4} = 5\frac{1}{4}$$

$$4 \times \frac{3}{4} = \frac{4}{1} \times \frac{3}{4} = \frac{12}{4} = 3$$

Practice
Find the product. Simplify, if necessary.

1. $8 \times \frac{2}{3}$ 2. $9 \times \frac{3}{8}$ 3. $6 \times \frac{3}{5}$ 4. $5 \times \frac{2}{5}$ 5. $3 \times \frac{7}{9}$

Multiplying Fractions

5.3 Planets and Stars

It is easy to confuse stars and planets in the night sky. One way to tell the difference between them is by their light. A planet's light shines steadily. How is this different from the light of a star?

To answer the question, find the products. Simplify, if necessary. Match each answer to one of the answer choices in the list after the problems. Then write the letter that corresponds to each answer in the space above its problem number at the bottom of the page. Some answers will be used more than once. Some letters are provided. You will need to divide the letters into words.

1. $6 \times \frac{1}{2}$ 2. $2 \times \frac{3}{8}$ 3. $15 \times \frac{1}{4}$ 4. $9 \times \frac{2}{3}$ 5. $5 \times \frac{1}{2}$

6. $\frac{5}{8} \times 7$ 7. $10 \times \frac{1}{4}$ 8. $\frac{5}{9} \times 9$ 9. $\frac{4}{9} \times 3$ 10. $12 \times \frac{1}{3}$

11. $\frac{7}{10} \times 2$ 12. $20 \times \frac{1}{5}$ 13. $\frac{5}{8} \times 3$ 14. $15 \times \frac{1}{3}$ 15. $\frac{4}{7} \times 9$

Answer Choices

$3\frac{3}{4}$ E $2\frac{1}{2}$ T $4\frac{3}{8}$ W $\frac{3}{4}$ H $5\frac{1}{7}$ R   6 A   5 L

$1\frac{2}{5}$ I   3 N $1\frac{7}{8}$ K   4 S $1\frac{1}{3}$ G

__ __ __ __ __   I   __ __ __   T   __ __ __ __ __ __ __
12 7 4 15 8   9 2 5   6 11 1 13 14 3 10

Multiplying Simple Fractions

The process of multiplying fractions is similar to the process of multiplying a fraction by a whole number.

$$\frac{3}{5} \times \frac{1}{4} = \frac{3}{20}$$

Multiply the numerators. Then multiply the denominators. Simplify, if necessary. (In this case, $\frac{3}{20}$ is simplified.)

$$\frac{2}{3} \times \frac{3}{4} = \frac{6}{12}$$

Multiply the numerators. Then multiply the denominators.

$$\frac{6}{12} = \frac{1}{2}$$

Simplify.

When multiplying some fractions, you can use a shortcut. The shortcut will often result in your answer being simplified.

$$\frac{\overset{1}{2}}{\underset{1}{3}} \times \frac{\overset{1}{3}}{\underset{2}{4}} = \frac{1}{2}$$

Find the greatest common factor of a numerator and a denominator, if possible. The greatest common factor of 2 and 4 is 2. Divide the first numerator and the second denominator by this factor. 2 ÷ 2 = 1 and 4 ÷ 2 = 2. Find the greatest common factor of the other numerator and denominator, if possible. The greatest common factor is 3. Divide the numerator and denominator by 3. 3 ÷ 3 = 1 and 3 ÷ 3 = 1. Multiply the new numerators and multiply the new denominators to find $\frac{1}{2}$. The product is simplified.

Here are more examples.

$$\frac{2}{3} \times \frac{4}{5} = \frac{8}{15}$$

$$\frac{3}{4} \times \frac{2}{7} = \frac{6}{28} = \frac{3}{14} \text{ or } \frac{3}{\underset{2}{4}} \times \frac{\overset{1}{2}}{7} = \frac{3}{14}$$

Practice

Find the products. Use the shortcut if possible. Simplify, if necessary.

1. $\frac{1}{2} \times \frac{3}{4}$
2. $\frac{2}{3} \times \frac{5}{8}$
3. $\frac{1}{3} \times \frac{4}{5}$
4. $\frac{5}{6} \times \frac{1}{3}$
5. $\frac{3}{4} \times \frac{4}{9}$

Multiplying Fractions

© Judith A. Muschla and Gary Robert Muschla

5.4 A Villain's Real Name

The Penguin has long been one of Batman's most dangerous adversaries. What is the Penguin's real name?

To answer the question, find the products. Simplify, if necessary. Match each answer to one of the answer choices in the list after the problems. Then write the letter that corresponds to each answer in the space above its problem number at the bottom of the page. One answer will be used more than once. One answer will not be used.

1. $\dfrac{3}{5} \times \dfrac{5}{6}$ 2. $\dfrac{5}{9} \times \dfrac{3}{10}$ 3. $\dfrac{5}{6} \times \dfrac{4}{5}$ 4. $\dfrac{1}{4} \times \dfrac{1}{2}$ 5. $\dfrac{7}{12} \times \dfrac{3}{8}$

6. $\dfrac{2}{3} \times \dfrac{7}{8}$ 7. $\dfrac{1}{2} \times \dfrac{3}{8}$ 8. $\dfrac{7}{10} \times \dfrac{2}{3}$ 9. $\dfrac{4}{5} \times \dfrac{2}{3}$ 10. $\dfrac{5}{6} \times \dfrac{3}{4}$

11. $\dfrac{1}{4} \times \dfrac{1}{5}$ 12. $\dfrac{3}{5} \times \dfrac{3}{4}$ 13. $\dfrac{3}{4} \times \dfrac{1}{5}$ 14. $\dfrac{1}{2} \times \dfrac{5}{6}$ 15. $\dfrac{3}{4} \times \dfrac{5}{8}$

Answer Choices

$\dfrac{5}{8}$ P $\dfrac{9}{20}$ W $\dfrac{2}{3}$ L $\dfrac{17}{24}$ N $\dfrac{7}{15}$ S $\dfrac{8}{15}$ I $\dfrac{7}{12}$ R

$\dfrac{3}{16}$ A $\dfrac{15}{32}$ B $\dfrac{1}{2}$ F $\dfrac{1}{20}$ H $\dfrac{7}{32}$ C $\dfrac{1}{6}$ T $\dfrac{3}{20}$ O

$\dfrac{5}{12}$ D $\dfrac{1}{8}$ E

____ ____ ____ ____ ____ ____   ____ ____ ____ ____ ____ ____ ____ ____ ____ ____ ____
13   8   12   7   3   14   5   11   4   8   2   4   6   1   9   4   3   14

____ ____ ____ ____ ____ ____ ____ ____ ____
 5   13   15   15   3   4   10   13   2

Multiplying Fractions

5.5 A Televised President

This president was the first to be televised. Who was he?

To answer the question, find the products. Simplify, if necessary. Match each answer to one of the answer choices in the list after the problems. Then write the letter that corresponds to each answer in the space above its problem number at the bottom of the page. Some answers will be used more than once. Some letters are provided. You will need to divide the letters into words.

1. $\dfrac{2}{9} \times \dfrac{3}{4}$
2. $\dfrac{7}{8} \times \dfrac{4}{7}$
3. $\dfrac{2}{3} \times \dfrac{1}{3}$
4. $\dfrac{3}{4} \times \dfrac{1}{2}$
5. $\dfrac{3}{5} \times \dfrac{1}{4}$

6. $\dfrac{4}{5} \times \dfrac{5}{8}$
7. $\dfrac{7}{10} \times \dfrac{3}{4}$
8. $\dfrac{6}{9} \times \dfrac{4}{5}$
9. $\dfrac{5}{10} \times \dfrac{3}{4}$
10. $\dfrac{3}{5} \times \dfrac{3}{4}$

11. $\dfrac{1}{3} \times \dfrac{4}{9}$
12. $\dfrac{6}{7} \times \dfrac{4}{5}$
13. $\dfrac{2}{3} \times \dfrac{4}{5}$
14. $\dfrac{3}{10} \times \dfrac{5}{12}$
15. $\dfrac{2}{7} \times \dfrac{5}{6}$

Answer Choices

$\dfrac{2}{9}$ S $\dfrac{1}{6}$ A $\dfrac{9}{20}$ O $\dfrac{3}{20}$ I $\dfrac{3}{8}$ L $\dfrac{24}{35}$ F $\dfrac{4}{27}$ T

$\dfrac{1}{8}$ V $\dfrac{8}{15}$ E $\dfrac{5}{21}$ K $\dfrac{1}{2}$ R $\dfrac{21}{40}$ N

__ __ __ __ __ __ __ __N__ __O__ __ __ __ __ __ __
12 6 1 7 15 9 5 2 10 3 8 14 13 4 11

© Judith A. Muschla and Gary Robert Muschla

Multiplying Fractions

Multiplying Fractions and Mixed Numbers

Before you can multiply a mixed number by a fraction, you must rename the mixed number as an improper fraction.

$2\frac{1}{3} \times \frac{1}{2}$

Rename the mixed number as an improper fraction. $2\frac{1}{3} = \frac{7}{3}$

$\frac{7}{3} \times \frac{1}{2} = \frac{7}{6}$

Multiply.

$\frac{7}{6} = 1\frac{1}{6}$

Simplify, if necessary, by renaming the improper fraction as a mixed number.

Here is another example.

$2\frac{3}{4} \times \frac{8}{9}$

Rename the mixed number as an improper fraction. $2\frac{3}{4} = \frac{11}{4}$

$\frac{11}{\underset{1}{4}} \times \frac{\overset{2}{8}}{9} = \frac{22}{9} = 2\frac{4}{9}$

Multiply. Use the shortcut. Then simplify.

Here are more examples.

$\frac{2}{5} \times 4\frac{2}{3} = \frac{2}{5} \times \frac{14}{3} = \frac{28}{15} = 1\frac{13}{15}$

$3\frac{1}{4} \times \frac{2}{7} = \frac{13}{\underset{2}{4}} \times \frac{\overset{1}{2}}{7} = \frac{13}{14}$

Practice

Find the products. Simplify, if necessary.

1. $1\frac{3}{4} \times \frac{2}{9}$

2. $\frac{3}{4} \times 2\frac{1}{2}$

3. $4\frac{3}{5} \times \frac{2}{3}$

4. $6\frac{1}{2} \times \frac{1}{4}$

5. $\frac{7}{8} \times 3\frac{1}{3}$

Multiplying Fractions

5.6 Famous Frontiersman

This man was born in Iowa in 1846. He became a Pony Express rider, scout, and showman. For almost 20 years he toured the country with his Wild West Show. Who was he?

To answer the question, find the products. Simplify, if necessary. Match each answer to one of the answer choices in the list after the problems. Then write the letter that corresponds to each answer in the space above its problem number at the bottom of the page. Some answers will be used more than once. Some letters are provided.

Multiplying Fractions

1. $4\frac{2}{5} \times \frac{1}{2}$

2. $3\frac{2}{3} \times \frac{1}{7}$

3. $2\frac{1}{2} \times \frac{1}{3}$

4. $5\frac{1}{4} \times \frac{1}{5}$

5. $\frac{1}{4} \times 3\frac{5}{8}$

6. $2\frac{3}{4} \times \frac{3}{8}$

7. $5\frac{1}{3} \times \frac{2}{3}$

8. $3\frac{3}{4} \times \frac{1}{3}$

9. $1\frac{2}{3} \times \frac{1}{2}$

10. $\frac{5}{6} \times 1\frac{1}{2}$

11. $\frac{7}{8} \times 2\frac{1}{2}$

12. $1\frac{3}{8} \times \frac{3}{4}$

13. $\frac{1}{4} \times 3\frac{2}{3}$

14. $6\frac{1}{3} \times \frac{3}{4}$

15. $\frac{1}{2} \times 9\frac{3}{8}$

Answer Choices

$2\frac{1}{5}$ A	$1\frac{1}{20}$ C	$2\frac{3}{16}$ Y	$\frac{5}{6}$ F	$3\frac{5}{9}$ M	$1\frac{1}{4}$ I
$4\frac{3}{4}$ W	$\frac{11}{21}$ O	$\frac{11}{12}$ B	$1\frac{1}{32}$ L	$\frac{29}{32}$ U	$4\frac{11}{16}$ D

___ ___ L ___ I ___ ___ " B ___ ___ ___ A L ___
14 10   6   1   7   5   3   9   2

___ ___ L ___" ___ O ___ ___
13 8   12   4   15 11

110

5.7 Honor to a President

This building in Washington, DC, was modeled after the Pantheon in Rome. It was built to honor one of our early presidents. What is the name of this building?

To answer the question, find the products. Simplify, if necessary. Match each answer to one of the answer choices in the list after the problems. Then write the letter that corresponds to each answer in the space above its problem number at the bottom of the page. Some answers will be used more than once. One answer will not be used. Some letters are provided. You will need to divide the letters into words.

1. $\dfrac{1}{6} \times 3\dfrac{1}{3}$ 2. $1\dfrac{3}{4} \times \dfrac{5}{6}$ 3. $\dfrac{1}{3} \times 4\dfrac{1}{2}$ 4. $\dfrac{1}{5} \times 3\dfrac{2}{3}$ 5. $1\dfrac{1}{2} \times \dfrac{3}{4}$

6. $2\dfrac{1}{4} \times \dfrac{1}{2}$ 7. $4\dfrac{3}{7} \times \dfrac{7}{8}$ 8. $\dfrac{2}{5} \times 3\dfrac{1}{3}$ 9. $2\dfrac{1}{3} \times \dfrac{2}{3}$ 10. $\dfrac{1}{9} \times 3\dfrac{3}{5}$

11. $1\dfrac{6}{7} \times \dfrac{2}{3}$ 12. $\dfrac{7}{8} \times 1\dfrac{1}{5}$ 13. $2\dfrac{3}{8} \times \dfrac{4}{7}$ 14. $3\dfrac{1}{9} \times \dfrac{1}{2}$ 15. $\dfrac{6}{7} \times 2\dfrac{1}{4}$

Answer Choices

$\dfrac{5}{9}$ **O** $1\dfrac{5}{14}$ **J** $1\dfrac{11}{24}$ **I** $\dfrac{11}{15}$ **R** $\dfrac{2}{5}$ **L** $1\dfrac{1}{20}$ **M**

$1\dfrac{1}{8}$ **E** $1\dfrac{1}{2}$ **N** $1\dfrac{13}{14}$ **H** $1\dfrac{2}{3}$ **W** $3\dfrac{7}{8}$ **A** $1\dfrac{5}{9}$ **F**

$1\dfrac{1}{3}$ **S** $1\dfrac{5}{21}$ **T**

$\underline{}$ $\underline{}$ $\underline{}$ $\underline{}$ $\underline{E}$ $\underline{}$ $\underline{}$ $\underline{E}$ $\underline{}$ $\underline{}$ $\underline{O}$ $\underline{}$
 11   15   5   13   9   14   4   8   3

$\underline{M}$ $\underline{}$ $\underline{}$ $\underline{}$ $\underline{R}$ $\underline{}$ $\underline{}$ $\underline{}$
 6   12   1   2   7   10

Multiplying Fractions

Multiplying Mixed Numbers

Before you can multiply mixed numbers, you must rename the mixed numbers as improper fractions.

$$1\frac{1}{3} \times 2\frac{1}{2}$$

$$\overset{2}{\frac{4}{3}} \times \frac{5}{\underset{1}{2}} = \frac{10}{3}$$

$$\frac{10}{3} = 3\frac{1}{3}$$

Rename the mixed numbers as improper fractions. $1\frac{1}{3} = \frac{4}{3}$ and $2\frac{1}{2} = \frac{5}{2}$.

Multiply the numerators and the denominators. Use the shortcut, if possible. 2 is the greatest common factor of the numerator 4 and the denominator 2. Simplify by renaming the improper fraction as a mixed number.

Here is another example.

$$2\frac{2}{3} \times 1\frac{3}{4}$$

$$\overset{2}{\frac{8}{3}} \times \frac{7}{\underset{1}{4}} = \frac{14}{3}$$

$$\frac{14}{3} = 4\frac{2}{3}$$

Rename the mixed numbers as improper fractions. $2\frac{2}{3} = \frac{8}{3}$ and $1\frac{3}{4} = \frac{7}{4}$.

Multiply the numerators and the denominators. Use the shortcut, if possible. 4 is the greatest common factor of the numerator 8 and the denominator 4. Simplify by renaming the improper fraction as a mixed number.

Here are more examples.

$$2\frac{1}{5} \times 3 = \frac{11}{5} \times \frac{3}{1} = \frac{33}{5} = 6\frac{3}{5}$$

$$4 \times 2\frac{3}{8} = \overset{1}{\frac{4}{1}} \times \frac{19}{\underset{2}{8}} = \frac{19}{2} = 9\frac{1}{2}$$

Practice
Find the products. Simplify, if necessary.

1. $3\frac{1}{2} \times 2\frac{1}{4}$ 2. $1\frac{3}{4} \times 2\frac{2}{3}$ 3. $2\frac{1}{3} \times 1\frac{1}{2}$ 4. $1\frac{1}{5} \times 4\frac{3}{8}$ 5. $4\frac{1}{4} \times 3\frac{3}{4}$

Multiplying Fractions

5.8 Big Cities

These two cities are the two most populous cities in the United States. What two cities are they?

To answer the question, find the products. Simplify, if necessary. Match each answer to one of the answer choices in the list after the problems. Then write the letter that corresponds to each answer in the space above its problem number at the bottom of the page. Some answers will be used more than once. Some letters are provided. You will need to divide the letters into words.

1. $2\frac{1}{7} \times 1\frac{1}{6}$ 2. $2\frac{1}{3} \times 5\frac{1}{4}$ 3. $2\frac{1}{3} \times 1\frac{2}{3}$ 4. $3\frac{1}{2} \times 3\frac{1}{2}$ 5. $2 \times 4\frac{1}{2}$

6. $3\frac{1}{2} \times 2\frac{1}{4}$ 7. $1\frac{1}{3} \times 2\frac{11}{12}$ 8. $2\frac{3}{4} \times 2\frac{2}{3}$ 9. $3\frac{1}{6} \times 2\frac{2}{3}$ 10. $4\frac{1}{2} \times 2\frac{1}{3}$

11. $1\frac{1}{3} \times 6\frac{1}{3}$ 12. $7\frac{1}{2} \times 1\frac{1}{3}$ 13. $1\frac{1}{2} \times 2\frac{4}{9}$ 14. $3\frac{3}{4} \times 1\frac{7}{9}$ 15. $4\frac{2}{3} \times 1\frac{1}{6}$

Answer Choices

$6\frac{2}{3}$ N $12\frac{1}{4}$ E   9 R $2\frac{1}{2}$ O   10 G $3\frac{8}{9}$ L

$8\frac{4}{9}$ S $3\frac{2}{3}$ W $7\frac{7}{8}$ D $5\frac{4}{9}$ Y $7\frac{1}{3}$ A $10\frac{1}{2}$ K

__ __ __ __ O __ __ A N __
14 4 13 15   5 10   6

__ __ __ __ N __ E __ __ __
7 1 11 8   12   3 2 9

5.9 Board Games

These two popular board games require players to create words using letters on tiles or dice. What are these two games?

To answer the question, find the products. Simplify, if necessary. Match each answer to one of the answer choices in the list after the problems. Then write the letter that corresponds to each answer in the space above its problem number at the bottom of the page. Some answers will be used more than once. One answer will not be used. Some letters are provided. You will need to divide the letters into words.

1. $1\frac{1}{4} \times 5\frac{1}{3}$ 2. $3\frac{3}{7} \times 2\frac{5}{8}$ 3. $2\frac{1}{2} \times 2\frac{1}{2}$ 4. $2\frac{1}{4} \times 2\frac{1}{2}$ 5. $1\frac{1}{3} \times 3\frac{1}{2}$

6. $2\frac{5}{7} \times 3\frac{1}{2}$ 7. $3\frac{3}{4} \times 1\frac{1}{2}$ 8. $6\frac{2}{3} \times 1\frac{1}{5}$ 9. $3\frac{3}{4} \times 1\frac{2}{3}$ 10. $7\frac{3}{5} \times 1\frac{1}{4}$

11. $1\frac{1}{4} \times 1\frac{1}{2}$ 12. $4\frac{3}{4} \times 3\frac{1}{5}$ 13. $2\frac{1}{2} \times 3\frac{1}{2}$ 14. $1\frac{1}{8} \times 1\frac{2}{3}$ 15. $1\frac{1}{2} \times 1\frac{2}{3}$

Answer Choices

9 **D**	$6\frac{1}{4}$ **E**	$9\frac{1}{2}$ **B**	$6\frac{2}{3}$ **O**	$4\frac{2}{3}$ **A**	8 **N**	$6\frac{1}{2}$ **P**
$5\frac{5}{8}$ **G**	$15\frac{1}{5}$ **C**	$2\frac{1}{2}$ **S**	$1\frac{7}{8}$ **L**	$8\frac{3}{4}$ **R**		

___ ___ ___ ___ ___ ___ ___ ___ A ___ ___ B ___ ___ ___ ___ ___
15   12   13   5   6   10   11   3   8   2   1   4   7   14   9

5.10 A Slow Swimmer

Despite its name, this organism is an animal. It lives in the ocean and uses its tentacles to swim very slowly, about 0.8 inches (2 cm) per minute. What is the name of this animal?

To answer the question, find the products. Simplify, if necessary. Match each answer to one of the answer choices in the list after the problems. Then write the letter that corresponds to each answer in the space above its problem number at the bottom of the page. Some answers will be used more than once. One answer will not be used. Some letters are provided.

1. $3\frac{4}{5} \times 1\frac{1}{4}$ 2. $2\frac{4}{9} \times 1\frac{1}{2}$ 3. $1\frac{2}{5} \times 3\frac{1}{3}$ 4. $2\frac{1}{2} \times 5\frac{3}{4}$ 5. $2\frac{5}{7} \times 1\frac{3}{4}$

6. $4\frac{1}{3} \times 3\frac{2}{3}$ 7. $3\frac{1}{3} \times 1\frac{2}{5}$ 8. $3\frac{1}{2} \times 2\frac{1}{2}$ 9. $1\frac{7}{20} \times 3\frac{1}{3}$ 10. $2\frac{1}{8} \times 2\frac{2}{3}$

11. $2\frac{1}{2} \times 1\frac{1}{2}$ 12. $4\frac{1}{2} \times 2\frac{1}{3}$ 13. $7\frac{1}{2} \times 1\frac{1}{6}$ 14. $3\frac{3}{4} \times 2\frac{4}{5}$ 15. $4\frac{4}{5} \times 3\frac{1}{3}$

Answer Choices

$15\frac{8}{9}$ E $4\frac{1}{2}$ B $5\frac{2}{3}$ T $4\frac{3}{4}$ C 16 S $4\frac{2}{3}$ N

$10\frac{1}{2}$ R $3\frac{3}{4}$ A $3\frac{2}{3}$ M $4\frac{1}{3}$ P $8\frac{3}{4}$ U $14\frac{3}{8}$ L

__ __ A __ S __ __ __ E __ T __ __ __
10 12   3   4 8 5   7   15 6 11

C __ __ U __ __ E __
13   1   2 9   14

Estimating the Products of Fractions

Estimating the products of fractions allows you to find approximate answers without multiplying the fractions. To estimate a product, follow the steps below.

Example: $\frac{3}{4} \times 2\frac{1}{3}$.

1. Round each fraction.

   $\frac{3}{4}$ can be rounded to 1.

   $2\frac{1}{3}$ can be rounded to 2.

2. Multiply.

   $1 \times 2 = 2$

   $$\frac{3}{4} \times 2\frac{1}{3} = \frac{\overset{1}{\cancel{3}}}{4} \times \frac{7}{\underset{1}{\cancel{3}}} = \frac{7}{4} = 1\frac{3}{4}$$

Compare your estimate to the product; 2 is a reasonable estimate because $2 \approx 1\frac{3}{4}$. The $\approx$ symbol means "is approximately equal to."

Here are more examples with their actual answers and estimates.

$$\frac{9}{10} \times \frac{7}{9} = \frac{7}{10} \qquad\qquad 2\frac{5}{6} \times 4\frac{1}{3} = 12\frac{5}{18} \qquad\qquad 1\frac{3}{4} \times 2\frac{1}{3} = 4\frac{1}{12}$$

$$1 \times 1 = 1 \qquad\qquad\qquad 3 \times 4 = 12 \qquad\qquad\qquad 2 \times 2 = 4$$

Practice

Find the products first. Then estimate to see if your answers are reasonable.

1. $\frac{5}{6} \times \frac{4}{5}$ 2. $1\frac{9}{10} \times \frac{5}{6}$ 3. $\frac{9}{10} \times 4\frac{1}{3}$ 4. $10\frac{1}{5} \times 3\frac{1}{3}$ 5. $4\frac{1}{5} \times 2\frac{7}{9}$

Multiplying Fractions

5.11 Big Teeth

Elephants are big animals and they have big teeth. About how much does a tooth of a fully grown elephant weigh?

To answer the question, estimate the products. If the given estimate for the problem is reasonable, write the letter for **yes** in the space above its problem number at the bottom of the page. If the estimate for the problem is not reasonable, write the letter for **no**. You will need to divide the letters into words.

1. $1\frac{3}{4} \times \frac{4}{5} \approx 2$ 2. $\frac{7}{8} \times 1\frac{1}{5} \approx 1$ 3. $6\frac{7}{8} \times 4\frac{6}{7} \approx 24$ 4. $\frac{6}{7} \times 20\frac{1}{3} \approx 20$

N. yes	**N.** yes	**T.** yes	**S.** yes
R. no	**O.** no	**E.** no	**D.** no

5. $1\frac{1}{6} \times 3\frac{2}{3} \approx 8$ 6. $5\frac{9}{10} \times 3\frac{3}{4} \approx 24$ 7. $2\frac{2}{3} \times 1\frac{3}{10} \approx 3$ 8. $15\frac{4}{5} \times 1\frac{5}{6} \approx 20$

U. yes	**V.** yes	**E.** yes	**N.** yes
O. no	**N.** no	**T.** no	**U.** no

9. $\frac{3}{4} \times 2\frac{3}{11} \approx 2$ 10. $12\frac{1}{4} \times 2\frac{2}{5} \approx 36$ 11. $4\frac{7}{10} \times 2\frac{2}{3} \approx 15$ 12. $1\frac{11}{12} \times 7\frac{5}{9} \approx 10$

P. yes	**T.** yes	**D.** yes	**W.** yes
C. no	**E.** no	**E.** no	**L.** no

__ __ __ __ __ __ __ __ __ __ __ __

10 12 7 6 3 1 9 5 8 2 11 4

Multiplying Fractions

5.12 Review: A First for TV

Electronic TV broadcasting began in 1928 with this character appearing on the screen. Who was he?

To answer the question, decide if the answers to the problems are correct. If the answer to a problem is correct, write the letter for **correct** in the space above the problem's number at the bottom of the page. If the answer is incorrect, write the letter for **incorrect**. One letter is provided. You will need to divide the letters into words.

1. $4\frac{18}{24}$ is simplified to $4\frac{3}{4}$.

   E. correct   **I.** incorrect

2. $20\frac{12}{8} = 21\frac{3}{4}$

   O. correct   **E.** incorrect

3. $7\frac{3}{4} = \frac{19}{4}$

   H. correct   **I.** incorrect

4. $7 \times \frac{3}{5} = 4\frac{1}{5}$

   L. correct   **G.** incorrect

5. $\frac{4}{5} \times \frac{7}{8} = \frac{7}{10}$

   T. correct   **E.** incorrect

6. $1\frac{3}{4} \times \frac{1}{2} = \frac{3}{4}$

   Y. correct   **T.** incorrect

7. $3\frac{1}{2} \times 2\frac{5}{7} = 9\frac{1}{2}$

   C. correct   **U.** incorrect

8. $1\frac{1}{2} \times 1\frac{1}{4} = 1\frac{5}{8}$

   T. correct   **X.** incorrect

9. $2\frac{3}{4} \times 2 = 5\frac{1}{4}$

   M. correct   **F.** incorrect

10. $7\frac{1}{7} \times 1\frac{1}{6} = 8\frac{1}{3}$

    A. correct   **S.** incorrect

Multiplying Fractions

$$\underline{\hspace{1cm}} \quad \underline{\hspace{1cm}} \quad \underline{\hspace{1cm}} \quad \underline{\hspace{1cm}} \quad \underline{\hspace{1cm}} \quad \underline{\hspace{1cm}} \quad \overset{H}{\underline{\hspace{1cm}}} \quad \underline{\hspace{1cm}} \quad \underline{\hspace{1cm}} \quad \underline{\hspace{1cm}} \quad \underline{\hspace{1cm}}$$
$$\quad 9 \qquad 1 \qquad 4 \qquad 3 \qquad 8 \qquad 6 \qquad\qquad 2 \qquad 7 \qquad 10 \qquad 5$$

Dividing Fractions

Many of the steps for dividing fractions are similar to the steps for multiplying fractions. The major difference is that you must change the divisor to its reciprocal, change the division sign to a multiplication sign, and then multiply.

Reciprocals are two numbers whose product equal 1. For example, the reciprocal of $\frac{1}{2}$ is $\frac{2}{1}$ because $\frac{1}{2} \times \frac{2}{1} = \frac{2}{2} = 1$. The whole number 3 can be written as $\frac{3}{1}$. The reciprocal of 3 is $\frac{1}{3}$ because $\frac{3}{1} \times \frac{1}{3} = \frac{3}{3} = 1$.

Dividing Whole Numbers and Fractions

When you divide fractions, you are separating (dividing) one group (quantity) into equal parts. For example, dividing 2 by $\frac{1}{2}$ is the same as finding how many $\frac{1}{2}$'s are in 2. This can be illustrated by taking two groups and showing the number of $\frac{1}{2}$'s.

□□   □□ $2 \div \frac{1}{2} = 4$

Follow these steps for dividing a whole number by a fraction. We will use the same example.

1. Write the whole number over 1. $\frac{2}{1}$

2. Write the problem. $\frac{2}{1} \div \frac{1}{2}$

3. Write the reciprocal of the divisor. $\frac{2}{1}$ (Hint: To write the reciprocal of any fraction, simply reverse the numerator and the denominator.)

4. Change the division sign to a multiplication sign. Multiply the numerators and multiply the denominators. $\frac{2}{1} \times \frac{2}{1} = \frac{4}{1}$

5. Simplify, if necessary. $\frac{4}{1} = 4$

Here are more examples. Use the shortcut for multiplying fractions when possible.

$$9 \div \frac{3}{5} = \frac{9}{1} \div \frac{3}{5} = \frac{\overset{3}{\cancel{9}}}{1} \times \frac{5}{\underset{1}{\cancel{3}}} = \frac{15}{1} = 15$$

$$\frac{2}{3} \div 4 = \frac{2}{3} \div \frac{4}{1} = \frac{\overset{1}{\cancel{2}}}{3} \times \frac{1}{\underset{2}{\cancel{4}}} = \frac{1}{6}$$

Practice
Find the quotients. Simplify, if necessary.

1. $2 \div \frac{2}{3}$ 2. $6 \div \frac{1}{5}$ 3. $\frac{3}{4} \div 2$ 4. $5 \div \frac{1}{4}$ 5. $\frac{4}{5} \div 3$

Dividing Fractions

6.1 A Grand Sight

It is said that Katharine Lee Bates wrote this song after looking out from Pikes Peak in Colorado. What song did Bates compose?

To answer the question, find the quotients. Simplify, if necessary. Match each answer to one of the answer choices in the list after the problems. Then write the letter that corresponds to each answer in the space above its problem number at the bottom of the page. Some answers will be used more than once. Some answers will not be used. Some letters are provided. You will need to divide the letters into words.

1. $3 \div \frac{1}{4}$ 2. $4 \div \frac{2}{3}$ 3. $\frac{2}{3} \div 3$ 4. $2 \div \frac{2}{3}$ 5. $\frac{7}{8} \div 4$

6. $2 \div \frac{1}{6}$ 7. $1 \div \frac{1}{3}$ 8. $12 \div \frac{1}{2}$ 9. $3 \div \frac{1}{5}$ 10. $\frac{3}{4} \div 2$

11. $\frac{1}{2} \div 10$ 12. $\frac{4}{5} \div 3$ 13. $\frac{5}{7} \div 3$ 14. $5 \div \frac{1}{3}$ 15. $\frac{7}{8} \div 2$

Answer Choices

$\frac{5}{21}$ **B**   15 **A**   6 **R**   12 **I** $\frac{2}{9}$ **U** $\frac{7}{16}$ **M** $\frac{3}{4}$ **P**

24 **C** $\frac{5}{8}$ **N**   3 **E** $\frac{1}{20}$ **F** $\frac{3}{8}$ **H** $\frac{7}{32}$ **T** $\frac{4}{15}$ **L**

$\overline{}$ $\overline{}$ $\overline{}$ $\overline{}$ $\overline{}$ $\overline{}$ $\overline{A}$ $\overline{T}$ $\overline{}$ $\overline{}$
14   15   7   2   6   8   10   4

$\overline{}$ $\overline{E}$ $\overline{}$ $\overline{U}$ $\overline{}$ $\overline{}$ $\overline{}$
13   9   5   1   11   3   12

Dividing Simple Fractions

Dividing two fractions is similar to dividing fractions and whole numbers.

$$\frac{3}{8} \div \frac{1}{2}$$

Rewrite the problem using the reciprocal of the divisor. Be sure to change the division sign to a multiplication sign.

$$\frac{3}{\underset{4}{8}} \times \frac{\overset{1}{2}}{1} = \frac{3}{4}$$

Multiply the numerators and multiply the denominators. Use the shortcut, if possible. Simplify, if necessary.

Here are more examples.

$$\frac{5}{9} \div \frac{2}{3} = \frac{5}{\underset{3}{9}} \times \frac{\overset{1}{3}}{2} = \frac{5}{6}$$

$$\frac{7}{8} \div \frac{3}{4} = \frac{7}{\underset{2}{8}} \times \frac{\overset{1}{4}}{3} = \frac{7}{6} = 1\frac{1}{6}$$

$$\frac{2}{3} \div \frac{2}{3} = \frac{\overset{1}{2}}{\underset{1}{3}} \times \frac{\overset{1}{3}}{\underset{1}{2}} = 1$$

Any number divided by itself equals 1.

Practice

Find the quotients. Simplify, if necessary.

1. $\frac{2}{3} \div \frac{3}{4}$ 2. $\frac{3}{5} \div \frac{2}{5}$ 3. $\frac{3}{8} \div \frac{1}{2}$ 4. $\frac{2}{3} \div \frac{5}{6}$ 5. $\frac{5}{6} \div \frac{2}{3}$

Dividing Fractions

6.2 Manhattan

Many places in America have been named after Native American words. Manhattan (in New York City) comes from an Algonquian word. What is thought to be the original meaning of this word?

To answer the question, find the quotients. Simplify, if necessary. Match each answer to one of the answer choices in the list after the problems. Then write the letter that corresponds to each answer in the space above its problem number at the bottom of the page. Some answers will be used more than once. One answer will not be used. Some letters are provided. You will need to divide the letters into words.

1. $\dfrac{5}{8} \div \dfrac{3}{4}$ 2. $\dfrac{3}{4} \div 3$ 3. $\dfrac{1}{3} \div \dfrac{4}{5}$ 4. $\dfrac{1}{6} \div \dfrac{2}{9}$ 5. $\dfrac{3}{10} \div \dfrac{1}{2}$

6. $\dfrac{3}{4} \div \dfrac{3}{10}$ 7. $\dfrac{3}{14} \div \dfrac{3}{8}$ 8. $\dfrac{4}{9} \div 2$ 9. $\dfrac{1}{2} \div \dfrac{4}{7}$ 10. $\dfrac{3}{25} \div \dfrac{1}{5}$

11. $\dfrac{4}{9} \div \dfrac{1}{4}$ 12. $\dfrac{1}{4} \div \dfrac{1}{2}$ 13. $\dfrac{2}{7} \div \dfrac{1}{2}$ 14. $\dfrac{5}{9} \div \dfrac{1}{3}$ 15. $\dfrac{8}{9} \div \dfrac{2}{3}$

Answer Choices

$\dfrac{3}{4}$ S $\dfrac{5}{6}$ D $1\dfrac{2}{3}$ H $\dfrac{1}{2}$ O $\dfrac{1}{4}$ G $2\dfrac{1}{2}$ E $1\dfrac{1}{4}$ Y

$1\dfrac{7}{9}$ N $1\dfrac{1}{3}$ W $\dfrac{5}{12}$ T $\dfrac{2}{9}$ R $\dfrac{7}{8}$ L $\dfrac{3}{5}$ I $\dfrac{4}{7}$ A

__ __ __ __ __ T __ __ T __ __ N __
10 4 12 9 7   6 1   14 5   2

I __ __ __ __ E __
11 15 13 3   8

6.3 Moisture in the Air

Air can hold moisture. When enough moisture builds up in the air, it will fall as precipitation. What term refers to the amount of moisture air can hold before precipitation falls?

   To answer the question, find the quotients. Simplify, if necessary. Match each answer to one of the answer choices in the list after the problems. Then write the letter that corresponds to each answer in the space above its problem number at the bottom of the page. Some answers will be used more than once. Some answers will not be used. One letter is provided.

1. $\dfrac{1}{12} \div \dfrac{1}{6}$ 2. $\dfrac{2}{3} \div \dfrac{5}{6}$ 3. $\dfrac{7}{9} \div \dfrac{2}{3}$ 4. $\dfrac{3}{8} \div \dfrac{1}{2}$ 5. $\dfrac{4}{7} \div \dfrac{1}{2}$

6. $\dfrac{1}{6} \div \dfrac{3}{10}$ 7. $\dfrac{2}{5} \div \dfrac{4}{5}$ 8. $\dfrac{5}{8} \div \dfrac{5}{6}$ 9. $\dfrac{1}{2} \div \dfrac{4}{7}$ 10. $\dfrac{1}{6} \div \dfrac{3}{4}$

11. $\dfrac{3}{5} \div \dfrac{9}{10}$ 12. $\dfrac{5}{9} \div \dfrac{5}{12}$ 13. $\dfrac{7}{8} \div \dfrac{7}{12}$ 14. $\dfrac{3}{4} \div \dfrac{3}{10}$ 15. $\dfrac{4}{9} \div \dfrac{2}{3}$

Answer Choices

$\dfrac{2}{9}$ **L** $\dfrac{1}{2}$ **I** $1\dfrac{1}{2}$ **Y** $1\dfrac{2}{3}$ **S** $\dfrac{3}{4}$ **E** $1\dfrac{1}{6}$ **A** $\dfrac{4}{5}$ **U**

$\dfrac{2}{3}$ **T** $2\dfrac{1}{2}$ **H** $1\dfrac{1}{7}$ **D** $\dfrac{5}{9}$ **V** $\dfrac{7}{8}$ **M** $2\dfrac{1}{3}$ **N** $1\dfrac{1}{3}$ **R**

__ __ __ __ __ __ __ __   __ __ __   I   __ __ __ __
12   8   10   3   11   1   6   4   14   2   9   5   7   15   13

Dividing Fractions and Mixed Numbers

When dividing fractions and mixed numbers, you must remember to first rename the mixed number as an improper fraction.

$3\frac{1}{4} \div \frac{1}{2}$ Rename the mixed number as an improper fraction. $3\frac{1}{4} = \frac{13}{4}$

$\frac{13}{4} \times \frac{2}{1}$ Change the divisor to its reciprocal and change the division sign to a multiplication sign.

$\frac{13}{\underset{2}{4}} \times \frac{\overset{1}{2}}{1} = \frac{13}{2}$ Multiply the numerators and multiply the denominators. Use the shortcut, if possible.

$\frac{13}{2} = 6\frac{1}{2}$ Simplify, if necessary.

Here are more examples.

$$1\frac{1}{3} \div \frac{1}{9} = \frac{4}{\underset{1}{3}} \times \frac{\overset{3}{9}}{1} = 12$$

$$\frac{7}{9} \div 2\frac{1}{3} = \frac{7}{9} \div \frac{7}{3} = \frac{\overset{1}{7}}{\underset{3}{9}} \times \frac{\overset{1}{3}}{\underset{1}{7}} = \frac{1}{3}$$

Practice

Find the quotients. Simplify, if necessary.

1. $3\frac{2}{3} \div \frac{2}{3}$ 2. $2\frac{3}{4} \div \frac{1}{8}$ 3. $\frac{4}{5} \div 2\frac{1}{10}$ 4. $\frac{3}{4} \div 6\frac{3}{8}$ 5. $4\frac{1}{6} \div \frac{5}{12}$

Dividing Fractions

6.4 First Televised World Series

The first televised baseball World Series aired in 1947. Who played and who won?

To answer the question, find the quotients. Simplify, if necessary. Match each answer to one of the answer choices in the list after the problems. Then write the letter that corresponds to each answer in the space above its problem number at the bottom of the page. Some answers will be used more than once. One answer will not be used. Some letters are provided. You will need to divide the letters into words.

1. $4\frac{1}{3} \div \frac{5}{6}$ 2. $3\frac{3}{4} \div \frac{5}{8}$ 3. $\frac{3}{8} \div 2\frac{1}{2}$ 4. $\frac{7}{9} \div 3\frac{1}{3}$ 5. $2\frac{3}{7} \div \frac{3}{14}$

6. $\frac{2}{3} \div 4\frac{1}{2}$ 7. $5\frac{2}{5} \div \frac{9}{10}$ 8. $\frac{4}{5} \div 1\frac{7}{10}$ 9. $1\frac{4}{9} \div \frac{5}{6}$ 10. $\frac{6}{7} \div 2\frac{2}{5}$

11. $\frac{4}{5} \div 3\frac{1}{3}$ 12. $4\frac{3}{5} \div \frac{2}{5}$ 13. $6\frac{2}{5} \div \frac{2}{3}$ 14. $7\frac{2}{3} \div \frac{2}{3}$ 15. $\frac{1}{2} \div 4\frac{1}{4}$

Answer Choices

$11\frac{1}{3}$ B $\frac{2}{17}$ K $\frac{3}{20}$ S $\frac{7}{30}$ H $9\frac{3}{5}$ Y   6 A

$\frac{4}{27}$ R $\frac{6}{25}$ N $5\frac{1}{5}$ O $\frac{8}{17}$ T $3\frac{2}{7}$ X $\frac{5}{14}$ G

$11\frac{1}{2}$ D $1\frac{11}{15}$ E

__ __ __ __ __ __E __ __ __E __ __T
13 7 11 15 9   3   5   2

__ __ __E __ __ __ __ __E __ __S
8 4   12 1 14 10   6

6.5 A Most Valuable Player

At the end of the season, the National Hockey League hands out an award for the season's most valuable player. What is this award called?

To answer the question, find the quotients. Simplify, if necessary. Match each answer to one of the answer choices in the list after the problems. Then write the letter that corresponds to each answer in the space above its problem number at the bottom of the page. Some answers will be used more than once. Some answers will not be used. Some letters are provided.

1. $1\frac{3}{5} \div \frac{3}{10}$ 2. $1\frac{1}{7} \div \frac{1}{14}$ 3. $\frac{1}{4} \div 1\frac{3}{8}$ 4. $4\frac{3}{4} \div 2$ 5. $3\frac{1}{7} \div \frac{1}{2}$

6. $3\frac{1}{2} \div \frac{7}{9}$ 7. $1\frac{1}{6} \div \frac{7}{32}$ 8. $1\frac{2}{3} \div \frac{3}{4}$ 9. $2\frac{7}{10} \div \frac{3}{7}$ 10. $3\frac{1}{3} \div \frac{5}{8}$

11. $4\frac{4}{7} \div \frac{8}{11}$ 12. $4\frac{3}{8} \div \frac{5}{6}$ 13. $\frac{1}{4} \div 1\frac{1}{3}$ 14. $1\frac{7}{9} \div \frac{4}{5}$ 15. $\frac{2}{5} \div 3\frac{2}{3}$

Answer Choices

$2\frac{2}{9}$ T $\frac{2}{11}$ I $5\frac{2}{3}$ N $2\frac{3}{8}$ P $6\frac{2}{7}$ H $\frac{7}{8}$ V

$5\frac{1}{3}$ R   16 E $4\frac{1}{2}$ O   18 S $6\frac{3}{10}$ L $\frac{6}{55}$ A

$5\frac{1}{4}$ M $\frac{3}{16}$ Y

```
__  __  __  __     __  __  M   __  __  __  A   __
11  15  10  14     12  2      6   1   3       9

__  __  O   __  __  __
 8   7      4   5  13
```

Dividing Mixed Numbers

Before you can divide mixed numbers, you must rename the mixed numbers as improper fractions. Once you have done that, follow the steps for dividing fractions.

$$1\frac{1}{4} \div 2\frac{1}{2}$$ Rename the mixed numbers as improper fractions. $1\frac{1}{4} = \frac{5}{4}$ and $2\frac{1}{2} = \frac{5}{2}$

$$\frac{5}{4} \div \frac{5}{2} = \frac{5}{4} \times \frac{2}{5} = \frac{\cancel{5}^{1}}{\cancel{4}_{2}} \times \frac{\cancel{2}^{1}}{\cancel{5}_{1}} = \frac{1}{2}$$ Change the divisor to its reciprocal and change the division sign to a multiplication sign. Multiply the numerators and multiply the denominators. Use the shortcut, if possible. Simplify, if necessary.

Here are more examples.

$$5\frac{1}{2} \div 2\frac{1}{4} = \frac{11}{2} \div \frac{9}{4} = \frac{11}{2} \times \frac{4}{9} = \frac{11}{\cancel{2}_{1}} \times \frac{\cancel{4}^{2}}{9} = \frac{22}{9} = 2\frac{4}{9}$$

$$5 \div 3\frac{1}{2} = \frac{5}{1} \div \frac{7}{2} = \frac{5}{1} \times \frac{2}{7} = \frac{10}{7} = 1\frac{3}{7}$$

Dividing Fractions

Practice
Find the quotients. Simplify, if necessary.

1. $8\frac{3}{4} \div 2\frac{1}{2}$ 2. $4\frac{1}{6} \div 3\frac{1}{3}$ 3. $7\frac{1}{2} \div 4$ 4. $3\frac{1}{2} \div 3\frac{1}{2}$ 5. $3\frac{2}{3} \div 1\frac{1}{2}$

6.6 The Center of the United States

Including Alaska and Hawaii, this place is the center of the United States. What place is this?

To answer the question, find the quotients. Simplify, if necessary. Match each answer to one of the answer choices in the list after the problems. Then write the letter that corresponds to each answer in the space above its problem number at the bottom of the page. Some answers will be used more than once. One answer will not be used. Some letters are provided. You will need to divide the letters into words.

1. $5\frac{3}{5} \div 4\frac{2}{3}$ 2. $8\frac{4}{9} \div 2\frac{2}{3}$ 3. $4\frac{1}{6} \div 1\frac{1}{4}$ 4. $6\frac{1}{2} \div 4\frac{1}{3}$ 5. $1\frac{1}{5} \div 4\frac{2}{3}$

6. $4\frac{1}{2} \div 1\frac{1}{3}$ 7. $5\frac{5}{8} \div 3\frac{3}{4}$ 8. $5 \div 1\frac{1}{2}$ 9. $1\frac{7}{9} \div 2\frac{2}{9}$ 10. $4\frac{1}{6} \div 1\frac{2}{3}$

11. $4\frac{8}{9} \div 3\frac{2}{3}$ 12. $9\frac{1}{2} \div 4$ 13. $3\frac{8}{9} \div 1\frac{2}{3}$ 14. $10\frac{1}{2} \div 3\frac{1}{2}$ 15. $4\frac{2}{3} \div 2\frac{2}{3}$

Answer Choices

$3\frac{1}{6}$ E $1\frac{3}{4}$ D $1\frac{1}{3}$ K $2\frac{1}{2}$ O $\frac{2}{3}$ R $1\frac{1}{5}$ A 3 S

$3\frac{1}{3}$ U $3\frac{3}{8}$ H $1\frac{1}{2}$ T $2\frac{3}{8}$ B $\frac{4}{5}$ Y $\frac{9}{35}$ N $2\frac{1}{3}$ C

$\frac{}{12}$ $\frac{U}{4}$ $\frac{T}{2}$ $\frac{}{13}$ $\frac{O}{8}$ $\frac{}{5}$ $\frac{T}{9}$ $\frac{}{}$

$\frac{}{14}$ $\frac{O}{3}$ $\frac{T}{6}$ $\frac{}{15}$ $\frac{}{1}$ $\frac{}{11}$ $\frac{}{10}$ $\frac{A}{7}$

Dividing Fractions

6.7 One Million Dollars

A million dollars is a lot of money. It weighs a lot, too. About how much does a million dollars in one-dollar bills weigh?

To answer the question, find the quotients. Simplify, if necessary. Match each answer to one of the answer choices in the list after the problems. Then write the letter that corresponds to each answer in the space above its problem number at the bottom of the page. Some answers will be used more than once. Some answers will not be used. Some letters are provided. You will need to divide the letters into words.

1. $4\frac{3}{8} \div 1\frac{1}{4}$
2. $4 \div 1\frac{2}{3}$
3. $2\frac{1}{4} \div 1\frac{2}{7}$
4. $7\frac{7}{8} \div 3\frac{1}{2}$
5. $8\frac{3}{4} \div 2\frac{1}{2}$

6. $8\frac{5}{9} \div 3\frac{2}{3}$
7. $5\frac{1}{5} \div 1\frac{19}{20}$
8. $3\frac{1}{5} \div 1\frac{1}{3}$
9. $5\frac{1}{4} \div 1\frac{1}{5}$
10. $4\frac{1}{5} \div 2\frac{2}{5}$

11. $9 \div 4\frac{1}{2}$
12. $11\frac{1}{4} \div 3$
13. $3 \div 1\frac{2}{7}$
14. $10 \div 3\frac{3}{4}$
15. $3\frac{1}{2} \div 2\frac{1}{3}$

Dividing Fractions

© Judith A. Muschla and Gary Robert Muschla

Answer Choices

$2\frac{2}{5}$ O	$2\frac{3}{4}$ E	$2\frac{1}{4}$ A	$1\frac{3}{4}$ N	$3\frac{1}{2}$ T	$2\frac{2}{3}$ D
$3\frac{3}{4}$ S	$1\frac{1}{2}$ P	$4\frac{3}{8}$ W	$2\frac{1}{3}$ U	2 H	$1\frac{2}{3}$ I

__ __ __ __ __ O __ __ __ __ __ __ __ __ S
1   9   8   5   11   6   12   4   3   7   15   2   13   10   14

6.8 Symbols of Political Parties

The Democratic Party and the Republican Party are the two major political parties in the United States. Each has an animal for a symbol. What is the symbol for the Democratic Party and the Republican Party, respectively?

To answer the question, find the quotients. Simplify, if necessary. Match each answer to one of the answer choices in the list after the problems. Then write the letter that corresponds to each answer in the space above its problem number at the bottom of the page. Some answers will be used more than once. One answer will not be used. Some letters are provided. You will need to divide the letters into words.

1. $3\frac{8}{9} \div 1\frac{2}{3}$ 2. $8\frac{2}{5} \div 3$ 3. $5\frac{1}{4} \div 1\frac{1}{5}$ 4. $5\frac{5}{6} \div 3\frac{1}{3}$ 5. $3\frac{1}{2} \div 1\frac{3}{4}$

6. $4\frac{2}{3} \div 3\frac{1}{2}$ 7. $4 \div 1\frac{3}{7}$ 8. $3\frac{8}{9} \div 2\frac{2}{9}$ 9. $7\frac{1}{3} \div 2$ 10. $8\frac{3}{4} \div 3\frac{1}{2}$

11. $4\frac{8}{9} \div 1\frac{1}{3}$ 12. $3\frac{3}{4} \div 1\frac{1}{14}$ 13. $7\frac{3}{4} \div 2\frac{1}{2}$ 14. $9\frac{5}{8} \div 2\frac{3}{4}$ 15. $7\frac{1}{3} \div 2\frac{2}{3}$

Answer Choices

$2\frac{1}{3}$ H $2\frac{3}{4}$ K 2 O $3\frac{1}{2}$ A $1\frac{3}{4}$ E $1\frac{2}{3}$ J $2\frac{4}{5}$ N

$2\frac{1}{2}$ L $3\frac{2}{3}$ D $4\frac{3}{8}$ P $1\frac{1}{3}$ Y $3\frac{1}{10}$ T

$\underline{}$ $\underline{}$ $\underline{}$ $\underline{}$ $\underline{}$ $\underline{}$ $\underline{}$ $\underset{\text{N}}{\underline{}}$ $\underset{\text{E}}{\underline{}}$ $\underline{}$ $\underline{}$ $\underline{}$ $\underline{}$ $\underline{}$ $\underline{}$
11 5 7 15 8 6 14   9   10 4 3 1 12 2 13

Dividing Fractions

Estimating Fraction Quotients
. . . .

Estimating fraction quotients helps you to find approximate answers without dividing the fractions.

Here is an example.

$$1\frac{4}{5} \div \frac{3}{4}$$

Follow the steps below to estimate the quotient.

1. Round each fraction.

   $1\frac{4}{5}$ can be rounded to 2.

   $\frac{3}{4}$ can be rounded to 1.

2. Divide.

   $2 \div 1 = 2$ $\qquad 1\frac{4}{5} \div \frac{3}{4} = \frac{9}{5} \div \frac{3}{4} = \frac{9}{5} \times \frac{4}{3} = \frac{\overset{3}{\cancel{9}}}{5} \times \frac{4}{\underset{1}{\cancel{3}}} = \frac{12}{5} = 2\frac{2}{5}$

2 is a reasonable estimate because $2 \approx 2\frac{2}{5}$. The $\approx$ symbol means "is approximately equal to."

Here are more examples with their actual answers and estimates.

$$\frac{7}{8} \div \frac{11}{12} = \frac{21}{22} \qquad\qquad 2\frac{9}{10} \div 1\frac{1}{5} = 2\frac{5}{12} \qquad\qquad 8\frac{1}{4} \div 3\frac{3}{4} = 2\frac{1}{5}$$

$$1 \div 1 = 1 \qquad\qquad\qquad 3 \div 1 = 3 \qquad\qquad\qquad 8 \div 4 = 2$$

Practice
Find the quotients first. Then estimate to see if your answers are reasonable.

1. $\frac{6}{7} \div \frac{7}{10}$
2. $3\frac{4}{5} \div 2$
3. $8\frac{3}{4} \div \frac{9}{10}$
4. $5\frac{5}{6} \div 3\frac{1}{3}$
5. $6\frac{2}{3} \div 6\frac{3}{4}$

Dividing Fractions

6.9 A Sleepy Head

This character in a Washington Irving short story slept for 20 years. Who was he?

To answer the question, estimate the quotients. If the given estimate for the problem is reasonable, write the letter for **yes** above its problem number at the bottom of the page. If the estimate for the problem is not reasonable, write the letter for **no**.

1. $11\frac{5}{8} \div 1\frac{4}{5} \approx 6$ 2. $5\frac{1}{4} \div 4\frac{3}{4} \approx 2$ 3. $7\frac{7}{10} \div \frac{7}{8} \approx 4$ 4. $21\frac{1}{3} \div 2\frac{6}{7} \approx 7$

N. yes	**S.** yes	**U.** yes	**I.** yes
I. no	**E.** no	**A.** no	**O.** no

5. $9\frac{1}{2} \div 1\frac{5}{6} \approx 9$ 6. $8 \div 3\frac{7}{9} \approx 2$ 7. $3\frac{7}{8} \div 2\frac{1}{4} \approx 2$ 8. $11\frac{3}{4} \div 1\frac{3}{4} \approx 6$

E. yes	**V.** yes	**L.** yes	**R.** yes
I. no	**D.** no	**E.** no	**T.** no

9. $\frac{7}{8} \div 1\frac{3}{10} \approx 1$ 10. $16 \div 3\frac{2}{3} \approx 4$ 11. $18\frac{9}{11} \div 4\frac{1}{5} \approx 3$ 12. $12\frac{1}{4} \div 2\frac{1}{8} \approx 4$

N. yes	**K.** yes	**M.** yes	**T.** yes
E. no	**S.** no	**P.** no	**W.** no

___ ___ ___   ___ ___ ___   ___ ___ ___ ___ ___ ___
 8   4   11   6   3   9   12   5   1   10   7   2

© Judith A. Muschla and Gary Robert Muschla

Simplifying Complex Fractions

A complex fraction is a fraction in which the numerator, the denominator, or the numerator *and* the denominator are fractions. To simplify a complex fraction, you must first divide the numerator by the denominator. (Remember that a fraction bar represents division.) Then simplify further, if necessary.

$$\frac{\frac{3}{4}}{6} \qquad \text{Divide } \frac{3}{4} \text{ by 6.}$$

$$\frac{3}{4} \div 6 = \frac{3}{4} \div \frac{6}{1} = \frac{\overset{1}{3}}{4} \times \frac{1}{\underset{2}{6}} = \frac{1}{8}$$

Here is an example using mixed numbers.

$$\frac{2\frac{1}{3}}{1\frac{1}{2}} \qquad \text{Write the mixed numbers as improper fractions and divide as you would two fractions. Simplify, if possible.}$$

$$2\frac{1}{3} \div 1\frac{1}{2} = \frac{7}{3} \div \frac{3}{2} = \frac{7}{3} \times \frac{2}{3} = \frac{14}{9} = 1\frac{5}{9}$$

Here are more examples.

$$\frac{\frac{2}{5}}{\frac{7}{9}} = \frac{2}{5} \div \frac{7}{9} = \frac{2}{5} \times \frac{9}{7} = \frac{18}{35} \qquad\qquad \frac{3\frac{2}{3}}{1\frac{2}{5}} = \frac{11}{3} \div \frac{7}{5} = \frac{11}{3} \times \frac{5}{7} = \frac{55}{21} = 2\frac{13}{21}$$

Practice

Simplify the complex fractions.

1. $\dfrac{\frac{1}{4}}{8}$ 2. $\dfrac{\frac{7}{7}}{\frac{7}{9}}$ 3. $\dfrac{9}{2\frac{2}{3}}$ 4. $\dfrac{\frac{3}{8}}{\frac{1}{2}}$ 5. $\dfrac{7\frac{3}{4}}{2\frac{1}{2}}$

Dividing Fractions

6.10 The Inventor of Baseball

Abner Doubleday is often given credit for inventing the game of baseball. But many sports historians believe a man other than Doubleday invented the game. Who was this man?

To answer the question, simplify the complex fractions. Match each answer to one of the answer choices in the list after the problems. Then write the letter that corresponds to each answer in the space above its problem number at the bottom of the page. Some answers will be used more than once. One answer will not be used. Some letters are provided.

1. $\dfrac{\frac{3}{2}}{3}$

2. $\dfrac{\frac{3}{4}}{5}$

3. $\dfrac{\frac{5}{8}}{\frac{3}{8}}$

4. $\dfrac{\frac{2}{1}}{8}$

5. $\dfrac{\frac{2}{3}}{\frac{4}{9}}$

6. $\dfrac{\frac{7}{8}}{1\frac{3}{4}}$

7. $\dfrac{6\frac{1}{3}}{2}$

8. $\dfrac{1\frac{7}{12}}{2\frac{3}{8}}$

9. $\dfrac{6}{2\frac{1}{3}}$

10. $\dfrac{2\frac{1}{4}}{1\frac{1}{2}}$

11. $\dfrac{10}{2\frac{1}{2}}$

12. $\dfrac{4\frac{2}{3}}{2\frac{2}{3}}$

13. $\dfrac{5\frac{1}{4}}{3}$

14. $\dfrac{\frac{1}{2}}{1\frac{1}{4}}$

15. $\dfrac{8\frac{3}{4}}{2\frac{1}{2}}$

Answer Choices

16 **A**	$3\frac{3}{4}$ **O**	$2\frac{4}{7}$ **H**	$\frac{2}{3}$ **D**	$\frac{3}{20}$ **I**	$1\frac{2}{3}$ **T**	$1\frac{1}{2}$ **E**
$\frac{2}{5}$ **C**	$1\frac{3}{4}$ **R**	$4\frac{1}{2}$ **N**	$3\frac{1}{6}$ **W**	$3\frac{1}{2}$ **X**	$\frac{1}{2}$ **G**	4 **L**

__ __ __ __ A __ __ __ __
4 11 5 15   1 8 10 12

__ A __ T __ R __ __ __ __
14 13 7 2 6 9 3

Expressing Fractions as Terminating or Repeating Decimals

Every fraction can be expressed as either a terminating or repeating decimal. An example of a terminating decimal is 0.25. An example of a repeating decimal is $0.\overline{3}$. The bar over the 3 indicates that the 3 repeats without end.

There are two methods you can use to express fractions as decimals. The first is to rewrite the fraction as an equivalent fraction with a denominator of 10, 100, 1,000, and so on. The fraction can then be changed directly to an equivalent decimal. But this method works only for fractions whose denominator is a factor of 10 or a factor of a power of 10. The second method is to divide the numerator of the fraction by its denominator. This method can be used to change any fraction to a decimal.

Method 1: Examples

To express $\frac{1}{2}$ as a decimal, multiply the numerator and denominator by the same number so that the denominator of the fraction equals 10. Then change the fraction to a decimal.

$$\frac{1}{2} \times \frac{5}{5} = \frac{5}{10} = 0.5$$

Because multiplying by $\frac{5}{5}$ is the same as multiplying by 1, the value of the fraction does not change. Here are two more examples.

$$\frac{1}{4} \times \frac{25}{25} = \frac{25}{100} = 0.25 \qquad \frac{1}{8} \times \frac{125}{125} = \frac{125}{1,000} = 0.125$$

Method 2: Examples

To express $\frac{1}{2}$ as a decimal, divide 1 by 2 and add a decimal point and a zero.

$$2\overline{)1.0}^{\,0.5} \qquad \frac{1}{2} = 0.5 \qquad 0.5 \text{ is a terminating decimal.}$$

Here is an example of a repeating decimal. To express $\frac{2}{9}$ as a decimal, divide 2 by 9, and add a decimal point and a zero.

$$
\begin{array}{r}
0.2 \\
9\overline{)2.0} \\
\underline{18} \\
2
\end{array}
$$

Because there is a remainder, add another zero. (Add more zeros, if necessary.)

$$
\begin{array}{r}
0.22 = 0.\overline{2} \\
9\overline{)2.00} \\
\underline{18} \\
20 \\
\underline{18} \\
2
\end{array}
$$

When it becomes clear that a digit or a group of digits repeats, write the decimal with a bar over the digit or digits that repeat.

Here are more examples using Method 2:

Express $\frac{3}{4}$ and $\frac{5}{6}$ as decimals.

$$\frac{3}{4}$$

$$
\begin{array}{r}
0.75 \\
4\overline{)3.00} \\
\underline{28} \\
20 \\
\underline{20} \\
0
\end{array}
$$

$$\frac{5}{6}$$

$$
\begin{array}{r}
0.833 = 0.8\overline{3} \\
6\overline{)5.000} \\
\underline{48} \\
20 \\
\underline{18} \\
20 \\
\underline{18} \\
2
\end{array}
$$

To express a mixed number as a decimal, keep the whole number and change the fraction to its decimal equivalent.

$$2\frac{1}{4} = 2.25 \qquad \left(\frac{1}{4} \times \frac{25}{25} = \frac{25}{100} = 0.25 \right)$$

Practice
Express each fraction as a decimal.

1. $\frac{3}{5}$ 2. $\frac{7}{8}$ 3. $\frac{5}{9}$ 4. $\frac{2}{11}$ 5. $3\frac{1}{2}$

Dividing Fractions

6.11 Connecticut

The name for the state of Connecticut comes from the Mohegan word *Quin-nehtukqut*. What was the original meaning of this word?

To answer the question, express each fraction as its decimal equivalent. Match each answer to one of the answer choices in the list after the problems. Then write the letter that corresponds to each answer in the space above its problem number at the bottom of the page. You will need to divide the letters into words.

1. $\dfrac{4}{5}$

2. $7\dfrac{3}{4}$

3. $\dfrac{3}{8}$

4. $4\dfrac{5}{8}$

5. $\dfrac{1}{6}$

6. $\dfrac{4}{15}$

7. $\dfrac{7}{25}$

8. $\dfrac{7}{9}$

9. $1\dfrac{5}{6}$

10. $\dfrac{6}{11}$

11. $1\dfrac{2}{3}$

12. $\dfrac{13}{50}$

13. $\dfrac{5}{12}$

14. $2\dfrac{1}{3}$

Answer Choices

$0.1\overline{6}$ **D**	$0.\overline{7}$ **T**	4.625 **H**	$1.8\overline{3}$ **L**	0.8 **I**	$1.\overline{6}$ **E**
$0.2\overline{6}$ **N**	0.375 **A**	7.75 **O**	0.28 **V**	$0.41\overline{6}$ **B**	
$2.\overline{3}$ **R**	$0.\overline{54}$ **S**	0.26 **G**			

___ ___ ___ ___ ___ ___ ___ ___ ___ ___ ___ ___ ___
13   11   10   1   5   11   8   4   11   9   2   6   12

___ ___ ___ ___ ___ ___ ___ ___ ___ ___
8   1   5   3   9   14   1   7   11   14

Changing Decimals to Fractions

You can change decimals to fractions by following these steps:

1. Find the place value of the last digit of the decimal.
2. Write the place value of the last digit as the denominator of the fraction.
3. Write the digits to the right of the decimal point as the numerator of the fraction.
4. Write any digits to the left of the decimal point as the whole number of the fraction.
5. Simplify the fraction, if possible.

Here are some examples:

$$0.7 = \frac{7}{10}$$

Because 7 is the last digit of the decimal and it is in the tenths place, 10 is the denominator of the fraction. Because 7 is to the right of the decimal point, 7 is the numerator of the fraction.

$$0.16 = \frac{16}{100} = \frac{4}{25}$$

Because 6 is the last digit of the decimal and it is in the hundredths place, 100 is the denominator of the fraction. Because 16 is to the right of the decimal point, 16 is the numerator of the fraction. This fraction can be simplified by dividing the numerator and denominator by 4, the greatest common factor of 16 and 100.

$$4.375 = 4\frac{375}{1,000} = 4\frac{3}{8}$$

Because 5 is the last digit of the decimal and it is in the thousandths place, 1,000 is the denominator of the fraction. Because 375 is to the right of the decimal point, 375 is the numerator of the fraction. Because 4 is to the left of the decimal, 4 is the whole number of the fraction. Again, the fraction is simplified using the greatest common factor.

Practice
Change each decimal to a fraction. Simplify the fraction, if possible.

1. 0.3　　　2. 0.75　　　3. 2.4　　　4. 0.008　　　5. 7.23

Dividing Fractions

6.12 NASA

NASA is the part of the United States government that is in charge of the exploration of space. What does the acronym NASA stand for?

To answer the question, change each decimal to a fraction in lowest terms. Match each answer to one of the answer choices in the list after the problems. Then write the letter that corresponds to each answer in the space above its problem number at the bottom of the page. One answer will not be used.

1. 1.4   2. 0.6   3. 1.42   4. 3.5   5. 0.25

6. 0.12   7. 1.875   8. 2.8   9. 0.375   10. 0.24

11. 1.75   12. 0.09   13. 0.5   14. 0.0625   15. 1.2

Answer Choices

$3\frac{1}{2}$ **I** $\frac{3}{8}$ **P** $1\frac{1}{5}$ **L** $\frac{1}{4}$ **S** $\frac{9}{100}$ **H** $1\frac{75}{100}$ **W**

$\frac{3}{5}$ **U** $\frac{3}{25}$ **A** $2\frac{4}{5}$ **E** $1\frac{3}{4}$ **T** $1\frac{2}{5}$ **O** $1\frac{7}{8}$ **R** $\frac{1}{2}$ **M**

$1\frac{21}{50}$ **C** $\frac{6}{25}$ **D** $\frac{1}{16}$ **N**

___ ___ ___   ___ ___ ___ ___ ___ ___ ___ ___
11 12   8   14   6   11   4   1   14   6   15

___ ___ ___ ___ ___ ___ ___ ___ ___ ___   ___ ___ ___
6   8   7   1   14   6   2   11   4   3   5   6   14 10

___ ___ ___ ___ ___
5   9   6   3   8

___ ___ ___ ___ ___ ___ ___ ___ ___ ___ ___ ___ ___ ___
6   10 13   4   14   4   5   11   7   6   11   4   1   14

Dividing Fractions

140

6.13 Review: The Yankees

The New York Yankees have a long and proud history as one of baseball's finest teams. But the Yankees were not always called the Yankees. What was the name of this New York baseball team before they became the Yankees?

To answer the question, decide if the answers to the problems are correct. If the given answer to a problem is correct, write the letter for **correct** in the space above the problem's number at the bottom of the page. If the answer is incorrect, write the letter for **incorrect**. One letter is provided.

1. $14 \div \dfrac{1}{2} = 7$

   R. correct
   E. incorrect

2. $\dfrac{5}{8} \div \dfrac{3}{4} = \dfrac{15}{32}$

   H. correct
   I. incorrect

3. $10 \div 2\dfrac{1}{2} = 4$

   S. correct
   X. incorrect

4. $\dfrac{7}{8} \div 1\dfrac{3}{4} = \dfrac{1}{2}$

   A. correct
   U. incorrect

5. $1\dfrac{7}{8} \div 1\dfrac{1}{4} = 1\dfrac{1}{2}$

   D. correct
   R. incorrect

6. Estimate: $11\dfrac{4}{5} \div 1\dfrac{1}{4} \approx 6$

   M. correct
   H. incorrect

7. $\dfrac{\frac{5}{9}}{2} = 1\dfrac{1}{9}$

   E. correct
   R. incorrect

8. $\dfrac{4\frac{2}{3}}{3\frac{1}{2}} = 1\dfrac{1}{3}$

   L. correct
   S. incorrect

9. $2\dfrac{1}{3} = 2.\overline{3}$

   H. correct
   T. incorrect

10. $\dfrac{7}{25} = 7.25$

    E. correct
    G. incorrect

$$\underline{\quad}\ \underline{\quad}\ \underline{\quad}\ \underline{\quad}\ \underline{\quad}\ \underline{\quad}\ \overset{N}{\underline{\quad}}\ \underline{\quad}\ \underline{\quad}\ \underline{\quad}\ \underline{\quad}$$

9   2   10   6   8   4   5   1   7   3

Dividing Fractions

Multiplying Signed Numbers

Numbers may be positive, negative, or zero. (Zero is neither positive nor negative.) Unless a number is represented with a negative sign, it is assumed to be positive.

Positive and negative numbers may be multiplied. When a negative number is a factor of a multiplication problem, the negative sign must be taken into account. Depending on the signs of the factors, the product may be positive or negative. Of course, if a factor is zero, the product is zero.

Multiplying Signed Numbers

Multiplying Two Integers

An integer may be positive, negative, or zero. For example, 3, −4, and 0 are integers. When multiplying integers, you must make sure that the product and its sign are correct.

Follow these rules for multiplying two integers:

1. If both integers are positive, the product is positive. (Remember that integers without signs are assumed to be positive.)

   $5 \times 3 = 15$

2. If both integers are negative, the product is positive.

   $-7 \times (-8) = 56$

3. If one integer is positive and the other is negative, the product is negative.

   $6 \times (-4) = -24$

4. If one of the integers is zero, the product is zero.

   $4 \times 0 = 0$ and $0 \times 4 = 0$ $-4 \times 0 = 0$ and $0 \times (-4) = 0$

   Here are more examples.

   $-4 \times 7 = -28$ $5 \times (-8) = -40$ $7 \times 3 = 21$ $-9 \times (-6) = 54$ $-9 \times 0 = 0$

Practice
Find the products.

1. $6 \times (-3)$ 2. 5×7 3. $-4 \times (-3)$ 4. $0 \times (-7)$ 5. -8×4

7.1 Going Shopping

The first department store in the United States opened here in 1868. In what city and state was this department store located?

To answer the question, find the products. Match each answer to one of the answer choices in the list after the problems. Then write the letter that corresponds to each answer in the space above its problem number at the bottom of the page. Some answers will be used more than once. Some answers will not be used. One letter is provided. You will need to divide the letters into words.

1. -7×9 2. $6 \times (-6)$ 3. $-5 \times (-6)$ 4. 6×4 5. -8×0

6. -9×3 7. -16×3 8. $2 \times (-7)$ 9. 2×12 10. $8 \times (-6)$

11. $-8 \times (-5)$ 12. $-6 \times (-7)$ 13. $-4 \times (-10)$ 14. 8×3 15. $5 \times (-9)$

Answer Choices

−48 L	−45 Y	−63 E	40 T	48 N	−36 I	24 A
−14 H	30 U	−40 M	−27 C	63 R	0 K	42 S

$$\underset{12}{\_\_}\ \underset{14}{\_\_}\ \underset{10}{\_\_}\ \underset{13}{\_\_}\ \underset{7}{\_\_}\ \underset{4}{\_\_}\ \underset{5}{\_\_}\ \underset{1}{\_\_}\ \underset{6}{\_\_}\ \underset{2}{\_\_}\ \ \underset{15}{\overset{T}{\_\_}}\ \underset{3}{\_\_}\ \underset{11}{\_\_}\ \underset{9}{\_\_}\ \underset{8}{\_\_}$$

Multiplying Signed Numbers

7.2 An Animated First

In 1914 Winsor McCay created the first animated cartoon. What was it titled?

To answer the question, find the products. Match each answer to one of the answer choices in the list after the problems. Then write the letter that corresponds to each answer in the space above its problem number at the bottom of the page. Some answers will be used more than once. Some answers will not be used. Some letters are provided. You will need to divide the letters into words.

1. $43 \times (-2)$ 2. $-18 \times (-2)$ 3. -10×9 4. $25 \times (-8)$ 5. -14×9

6. $15 \times (-6)$ 7. $-11 \times (-9)$ 8. -12×10 9. $-25 \times (-5)$ 10. 24×8

11. $20 \times (-6)$ 12. -25×17 13. -28×0 14. $-12 \times (-16)$ 15. $24 \times (-34)$

Answer Choices

125 **D**	–99 **Y**	–86 **O**	0 **N**	–90 **E**	–200 **I**
–816 **U**	–120 **R**	36 **A**	99 **H**	200 **J**	192 **T**
–126 **S**	–425 **G**				

___ ___ ___ ___ ___ __E__ ___ ___ ___ __I__ ___ ___ ___ ___ ___

12 6 8 14 4   10 7 3 9   13 1 5 2 15 11

© Judith A. Muschla and Gary Robert Muschla

Multiplying More Than Two Integers

You can use either of two methods to find the correct sign when multiplying more than two integers.

Method 1
1. Work from left to right.
2. Multiply the integers two at a time.
3. Follow the rules for multiplying two integers to find the correct sign.

$-4 \times 3 \times (-2)$ Multiply -4×3 to find -12.

$-12 \times (-2) = 24$ Multiply -12 by -2 to find 24.

Method 2
1. Find the product of the factors.
2. If all the numbers you multiply are positive, the sign of the product is positive.
3. If there is an odd number of negative factors, the sign of the product is negative.
4. If there is an even number of negative factors, the sign of the product is positive.

$-3 \times (-2) \times 4 = 24$ Because there is an even number of negative factors, the sign of the product is positive.

$-5 \times (-2) \times (-1) \times 4 = -40$ Because there is an odd number of negative factors, the sign of the product is negative.

Remember that the product of any integers multiplied by zero equals zero.

$-4 \times 0 \times (-7) \times 2 = 0$

Practice
Find the products.

1. $6 \times (-3) \times (-2)$

2. $-4 \times (-3) \times (-1)$

3. $7 \times (-4) \times (-1) \times 2$

4. $8 \times (-1) \times (-2) \times (-4)$

7.3 Musical Instruments

Musical instruments are grouped according to the ways they make sounds. What are the four major groups of musical instruments?

To answer the question, find the products. Match each answer to one of the answer choices in the list after the problems. Then write the letter that corresponds to each answer in the space above its problem number at the bottom of the page. One answer will not be used.

1. $-3 \times (-2) \times (-4)$

2. $7 \times 4 \times (-2)$

3. $4 \times 0 \times 3 \times 2$

4. $-8 \times 2 \times (-1) \times 2$

5. $6 \times (-5) \times 2$

6. $-2 \times (-3) \times 1 \times 4$

7. $-5 \times (-2) \times 3 \times (-1)$

8. $4 \times 3 \times 2 \times (-2)$

9. $7 \times (-3) \times (-1) \times 2$

10. $-3 \times (-3) \times 2 \times 1 \times (-4)$

11. $4 \times (-5) \times 2 \times (-1)$

12. $-10 \times (-2) \times 4 \times 1$

13. $7 \times (-3) \times (-1) \times (-2) \times (-4)$

14. $4 \times 2 \times 8 \times (-3) \times 1$

15. $-2 \times (-1) \times 3 \times (-4) \times 5$

Answer Choices

80 N	−24 I	168 P	0 A	42 C	32 E	−192 S
−56 U	−30 D	−120 W	−48 R	−72 O	24 G	−60 T
72 F	40 B					

___ ___ ___ ___ ___   ___ ___ ___ ___ ___ ___ ___
11   8   3   14 14   14   5   8   1   12   6   14

___ ___ ___ ___ ___ ___ ___ ___ ___ ___   ___ ___ ___ ___ ___ ___ ___ ___ ___
13   4   8   9   2   14 14   1   10 12   15 10 10   7   15   1   12   7   14

Evaluating Integers with Exponents

An exponent shows the number of times a base is used as a factor. For example, in 3^2, 3 is the base and 2 is the exponent. $3^2 = 3 \times 3 = 9$

Following are examples of bases and exponents along with their equivalents.

- 3^0 is read "3 to the zero power" and is equal to 1. Any positive or negative number raised to the zero power equals 1.

- 4^1 is read "4 to the first power" and is equal to 4.

- 6^2 is read "6 to the second power" or "6 squared" and is equal to 36.

- 5^3 is read "5 to the third power" or "5 cubed" and is equal to 125.

- $(-2)^4$ means that –2 is the base and it is raised to the fourth power and is equal to 16.

- -2^4 is the opposite of 2 to the fourth power and is equal to –16.

Evaluating integers with exponents requires extra care. Pay close attention to whether the negative integer is raised to the power or the whole expression is negative.

Here are more examples.

$$9^2 = 9 \times 9 = 81 \qquad 4^3 = 4 \times 4 \times 4 = 64$$
$$(-7)^2 = -7 \times (-7) = 49 \qquad -7^2 = -(7 \times 7) = -49$$

Practice
Evaluate the following.

1. 4^2 2. 7^3 3. -5^2 4. $(-5)^2$ 5. 8^1

Multiplying Signed Numbers

7.4 A Great Sport Event

This is site of the world's largest spectator sport event. What is it?

To answer the question, evaluate each integer with its exponent. Match each answer to one of the answer choices in the list after the problems. Then write the letter that corresponds to each answer in the space above its problem number at the bottom of the page. One answer will not be used. You will need to divide the letters into words.

1. -4^3 2. -2^4 3. $(-2)^0$ 4. -1^2 5. 3^5

6. $(-5)^3$ 7. 8^2 8. 5^3 9. -6^2 10. -2^8

11. -5^2 12. 10^3 13. $(-2)^8$ 14. 12^1 15. -2^5

Answer Choices

−16 P	1,000 Y	−1 R	−36 O	125 W	−25 H
1 N	64 M	243 D	−32 L	12 I	−125 S	256 E
16 C	−64 T	−256 A			

___ ___ ___ ___ ___ ___ ___ ___ ___ ___ ___ ___ ___ ___ ___
 1   11 13 14   3   5   14 10   3   10   2   9   15 14   6

___ ___ ___ ___ ___ ___ ___ ___ ___ ___ ___ ___ ___
 7   9   1   9   4   6   2   13 13   5   8   10 12

Multiplying Two Rational Numbers

Rational numbers are the set of all numbers that can be represented in the form $\frac{a}{b}$, where a and b are integers and $b \neq 0$. When multiplying signed rational numbers, you must place the correct sign in the product. This process is the same as for multiplying signed integers.

Follow these guidelines:

- A positive number × a positive number = a positive number.

- A positive number × a negative number = a negative number.

- A negative number × a positive number = a negative number.

- A negative number × a negative number = a positive number.

- Any number × zero = zero.

$$-\frac{2}{3} \times \frac{1}{3} = -\frac{2}{9}$$

Multiply the numerators and multiply the denominators. Because a negative number was multiplied by a positive number, the sign of the product is negative.

$$3\frac{1}{2} \times \left(-1\frac{1}{3}\right)$$

$$\frac{7}{\underset{1}{2}} \times \left(-\frac{\overset{2}{4}}{3}\right) = -\frac{14}{3} = -4\frac{2}{3}$$

Rename the mixed numbers as improper fractions. Multiply the numerators and multiply the denominators. Use the shortcut, if possible. Simplify. Because a positive number was multiplied by a negative number, the sign of the product is negative.

$$-1\frac{1}{6} \times \left(-1\frac{1}{2}\right) = -\frac{7}{\underset{2}{6}} \times \left(-\frac{\overset{1}{3}}{2}\right) = \frac{7}{4} = 1\frac{3}{4}$$

Because two negative numbers were multiplied, the sign of the product is positive.

Practice
Find the products. Simplify, if necessary.

1. $-\frac{4}{5} \times \left(-\frac{2}{3}\right)$ 2. $5\frac{2}{5} \times \left(-\frac{2}{9}\right)$ 3. $-2\frac{1}{3} \times 1\frac{2}{3}$ 4. $-3 \times \left(-3\frac{1}{3}\right)$ 5. $3\frac{1}{2} \times \left(-1\frac{1}{4}\right)$

7.5 Nicknames for Massachusetts

Two nicknames for Massachusetts are the Bay State and the Baked Bean State. What is a third nickname?

To answer the question, find the products. Simplify, if necessary. Match each answer to one of the answer choices in the list after the problems. Then write the letter that corresponds to each answer in the space above its problem number at the bottom of the page. Some answers will be used more than once. Some answers will not be used. Some letters are provided. You will need to divide the letters into words.

1. $-\frac{2}{3} \times \frac{2}{3}$
2. $\frac{2}{3} \times \left(-\frac{4}{5}\right)$
3. $\frac{3}{4} \times \frac{2}{3}$
4. $\frac{3}{4} \times \left(-2\frac{2}{3}\right)$
5. $-3 \times \left(-\frac{1}{6}\right)$

6. $-\frac{5}{6} \times \left(-1\frac{1}{2}\right)$
7. $\frac{5}{6} \times \left(-\frac{4}{5}\right)$
8. $\frac{2}{3} \times \left(-2\frac{1}{2}\right)$
9. $-\frac{2}{5} \times 1\frac{2}{3}$
10. $-2\frac{5}{6} \times \left(-1\frac{1}{2}\right)$

11. $2\frac{2}{3} \times 1\frac{3}{4}$
12. $-1\frac{1}{9} \times 1\frac{1}{2}$
13. $-1\frac{3}{4} \times \left(-3\frac{1}{2}\right)$

14. $-3\frac{1}{2} \times \left(-1\frac{1}{3}\right)$
15. $-1\frac{1}{3} \times \left(-3\frac{2}{3}\right)$

Answer Choices

$-\frac{2}{3}$ **E** $-\frac{4}{9}$ **N** $4\frac{1}{4}$ **A** $\frac{1}{2}$ **O** -2 **Y** $-\frac{8}{15}$ **D**

$12\frac{3}{4}$ **P** $4\frac{8}{9}$ **H** $1\frac{1}{4}$ **S** $4\frac{2}{3}$ **T** $-\frac{3}{4}$ **M** $-1\frac{2}{3}$ **L**

$-1\frac{1}{4}$ **V** $6\frac{1}{8}$ **C**

$\underline{\quad}$ $\underline{\quad}$ $\underline{\quad}$ $\underline{\quad}$ $\underline{\quad}$ $\underline{\quad}$ $\underline{\quad}$ $\underset{O}{\underline{\quad}}$ $\underline{\quad}$ $\underline{\quad}$ $\underline{\quad}$ $\underline{\quad}$ $\underset{T}{\underline{\quad}}$ $\underline{\quad}$ $\underline{\quad}$ $\underline{\quad}$

14 15 9 5 12 2 13   8 3 1 4 6   10 11 7

7.6 Underdog

Underdog is a famous cartoon hero. What was Underdog's girlfriend's name?

To answer the question, find the products. Simplify, if possible. Match each answer to one of the answer choices in the list after the problems. Then write the letter that corresponds to each answer in the space above its problem number at the bottom of the page. Some answers will be used more than once. Some answers will not be used. Some letters are provided. You will need to divide the letters into words.

1. $4\frac{1}{6} \times \left(-1\frac{4}{5}\right)$ 2. $-1\frac{1}{2} \times \left(-2\frac{4}{9}\right)$ 3. $-3\frac{1}{2} \times 2\frac{1}{2}$ 4. $-3\frac{4}{5} \times \left(-1\frac{1}{4}\right)$

5. $4\frac{1}{2} \times 2\frac{1}{3}$ 6. $7 \times \left(-1\frac{1}{4}\right)$ 7. $-1\frac{3}{4} \times 3$ 8. $1\frac{1}{5} \times 4\frac{2}{3}$

9. $1\frac{1}{4} \times \left(-3\frac{1}{3}\right)$ 10. $-2\frac{2}{5} \times \left(-2\frac{1}{3}\right)$ 11. $-1\frac{1}{2} \times 2\frac{1}{3}$ 12. $2\frac{4}{5} \times \left(-1\frac{1}{4}\right)$

13. $-1\frac{2}{3} \times \left(-3\frac{1}{2}\right)$ 14. $-2\frac{2}{3} \times 2\frac{3}{4}$ 15. $-2\frac{5}{7} \times \left(-3\frac{1}{2}\right)$

Answer Choices

$4\frac{3}{4}$ T $-7\frac{1}{2}$ O $-3\frac{2}{3}$ N $-4\frac{1}{6}$ L $5\frac{3}{5}$ P $7\frac{2}{3}$ K

$-5\frac{1}{4}$ Y $-3\frac{1}{2}$ R $9\frac{1}{2}$ W $-8\frac{3}{4}$ E $-7\frac{1}{3}$ S $10\frac{1}{2}$ B

$3\frac{2}{3}$ U $5\frac{5}{6}$ D

__	__	E	__	__	__	__	L	__	__	__	__	E	__	__	__
14	15	3	4	8	1	9	7	10	2	11	5	12	6	13	

7.7 Review: A Grand Old Sport

This is the longest-running sporting event in the United States. What is it?

To answer the question, decide if the answers to the problems are correct. If the given answer is correct, write the letter for **correct** in the space above the problem's number at the bottom of the page. If the answer is incorrect, write the letter for **incorrect**. Some letters are provided. You will need to divide the letters into words.

1. $9 \times (-3) = -27$

2. $-16 \times (-4) = -64$

3. $-31 \times 0 = -31$

U. correct	**R.** correct	**M.** correct
E. incorrect	**Y.** incorrect	**E.** incorrect

4. $-7 \times (-2) \times 1 \times (-3) = 42$

5. $-2^4 = -16$

6. $(-5)^2 = 25$

S. correct	**N.** correct	**H.** correct
Y. incorrect	**R.** incorrect	**E.** incorrect

7. $-1^3 = -3$

8. $-\dfrac{1}{2} \times \left(-\dfrac{5}{9}\right) = -\dfrac{5}{18}$

9. $4 \times \left(-\dfrac{3}{4}\right) = -3$

N. correct	**E.** correct	**E.** correct
C. incorrect	**B.** incorrect	**Y.** incorrect

10. $-2 \times 1\dfrac{3}{4} = 3\dfrac{1}{2}$

11. $2\dfrac{1}{2} \times \left(-2\dfrac{1}{2}\right) = -6\dfrac{1}{4}$

12. $-2\dfrac{2}{3} \times \left(-3\dfrac{1}{6}\right) = 8\dfrac{4}{9}$

M. correct	**K.** correct	**D.** correct
K. incorrect	**B.** incorrect	**R.** incorrect

T __ __ __ E __ T __ __ __ __ __ __ __ R __ __
  6 9 11   5   1 7 10 2 12 3   8 4

© Judith A. Muschla and Gary Robert Muschla

Dividing Signed Numbers

Dividing signed numbers is the inverse (opposite) of multiplying signed numbers. Depending on the signs and numbers of the divisor and dividend, the quotient may be positive, negative, or zero. The divisor cannot equal zero, because division by zero is undefined.

Dividing Integers

When dividing integers, you must make sure that the sign of the quotient is correct.

Follow these rules for dividing signed integers:

- If the divisor and the dividend are positive, the sign of the quotient is positive.

  $10 \div 2 = 5$

- If both the divisor and the dividend are negative, the sign of the quotient is positive.

  $-6 \div (-3) = 2$

- If either the divisor or the dividend is negative and the other is positive, the quotient is negative.

  $-12 \div 4 = -3$ and $12 \div (-4) = -3$

- If the dividend is zero and the divisor is any number other than zero, the quotient is zero.

  $0 \div 7 = 0$ and $0 \div (-7) = 0$

- Division by zero is undefined.

  Here are more examples.

  $-18 \div 9 = -2$ $21 \div (-7) = -3$ $8 \div 4 = 2$ $-14 \div (-2) = 7$ $-16 \div 4 = -4$

Dividing Signed Numbers

Practice
Find the quotients.

1. $24 \div (-6)$ 2. $-15 \div (-3)$ 3. $12 \div 6$ 4. $-10 \div 5$ 5. $-30 \div (-5)$

8.1 A Long Coastline

The coastline of Alaska is longer than the coastlines of all the other states combined. About how many miles is the coastline of Alaska?

To answer the question, find the quotients. Match each answer to one of the answer choices in the list after the problems. Then write the letter that corresponds to each answer in the space above its problem number at the bottom of the page. Some answers will not be used. You will need to divide the letters into words.

1. −12 ÷ 4   2. 8 ÷ (−2)   3. 24 ÷ 3   4. −18 ÷ (−3)   5. 0 ÷ 9

6. 45 ÷ (−5)   7. 28 ÷ 4   8. 99 ÷ (−9)   9. 10 ÷ (−2)   10. −20 ÷10

11. −30 ÷ 3   12. −32 ÷ (−8)   13. −36 ÷ 6   14. 81 ÷ 9

Answer Choices

−4 N	7 R	−2 F	−3 U	−6 S	5 W	8 I	9 X
−5 H	0 E	6 O	−9 T	−11 A	−10 Y	2 M	4 D

___ ___ ___ ___ ___ ___ ___ ___ ___ ___ ___
13 3 14 6 9 4 1 13 8 2 12

___ ___ ___ ___ ___ ___ ___ ___ ___ ___ ___ ___ ___ ___ ___
13 3 14 9 1 2 12 7 5 12 10 4 7 6 11

8.2 Taste Zones

Your tongue has four major taste zones. What are they?

To answer the question, find the quotients. Match each answer to one of the answer choices in the list after the problems. Then write the letter that corresponds to each answer in the space above its problem number at the bottom of the page. Some answers will be used more than once. Some answers will not be used. Some letters are provided. You will need to divide the letters into words.

1. $65 \div (-5)$ 2. $42 \div (-3)$ 3. $92 \div 4$ 4. $-90 \div 10$

5. $77 \div 11$ 6. $-125 \div (-5)$ 7. $81 \div (-9)$ 8. $-210 \div (-30)$

9. $-120 \div (-6)$ 10. $-45 \div 15$ 11. $168 \div (-21)$ 12. $-99 \div (-33)$

13. $160 \div 8$ 14. $60 \div (-12)$ 15. $-250 \div (-25)$

Answer Choices

20 E	−8 W	−13 O	10 I	7 T	5 N	−3 U
25 Y	−5 B	−10 H	−9 S	23 R	3 L	−14 A

```
__  __  __  T   __  __  S  __  __  R
14  15   8       9   3     1  10

__  __  __  T   __  __  __  E  __  __
 4   2  12       6   7  11     13   5
```

© Judith A. Muschla and Gary Robert Muschla

Dividing Rational Numbers

When dividing rational numbers, you must place the correct sign in the quotient. This process is the same as for dividing integers.

Follow these guidelines:

- A positive number ÷ by a positive number = a positive number.

- A positive number ÷ by a negative number = a negative number.

- A negative number ÷ by a positive number = a negative number.

- A negative number ÷ by a negative number = a positive number.

- Zero ÷ by any number = zero.

- Any number ÷ by zero is undefined.

$$-\frac{5}{9} \div \frac{2}{3}$$

$$-\frac{5}{9} \times \frac{3}{2}$$

Rewrite the problem using the reciprocal of the divisor. Change the division sign to a multiplication sign.

$$-\frac{5}{\overset{}{\underset{3}{9}}} \times \frac{\overset{1}{3}}{2} = -\frac{5}{6}$$

Multiply the numerators and multiply the denominators. Use the shortcut, if possible. Simplify, if necessary. Because a negative number was divided by a positive number, the sign of the quotient is negative.

$$-1\frac{1}{4} \div \left(-3\frac{1}{2}\right)$$

Rename the mixed numbers as improper fractions. $-1\frac{1}{4} = -\frac{5}{4}$ and $-3\frac{1}{2} = -\frac{7}{2}$

$$-\frac{5}{4} \div \left(-\frac{7}{2}\right) = -\frac{5}{\underset{2}{4}} \times \left(-\frac{\overset{1}{2}}{7}\right) = \frac{5}{14}$$

Change the divisor to its reciprocal and change the division sign to a multiplication sign. Multiply the numerators and multiply the denominators. Use the shortcut, if possible. Simplify, if necessary. Because a negative number was divided by a negative number, the sign of the quotient is positive.

Practice
Find the quotients. Simplify, if necessary.

1. $-\frac{1}{8} \div \frac{3}{4}$ 2. $\frac{2}{3} \div \frac{4}{5}$ 3. $-1\frac{1}{3} \div \left(-\frac{2}{3}\right)$ 4. $-7\frac{1}{2} \div 3$ 5. $-4\frac{2}{3} \div 2\frac{2}{3}$

Dividing Signed Numbers

8.3 Horse Racing Through the Ages

Dividing Signed Numbers

1. $-\dfrac{1}{4} \div \left(-\dfrac{3}{4}\right)$

2. $-\dfrac{9}{20} \div \dfrac{3}{5}$

3. $\dfrac{3}{5} \div \left(-\dfrac{9}{10}\right)$

4. $\dfrac{3}{10} \div \left(-\dfrac{2}{3}\right)$

5. $\dfrac{8}{9} \div \left(-\dfrac{1}{3}\right)$

6. $-\dfrac{1}{2} \div \left(-\dfrac{4}{5}\right)$

7. $-\dfrac{2}{5} \div \dfrac{4}{5}$

8. $-3\dfrac{3}{4} \div 2\dfrac{1}{2}$

9. $1\dfrac{1}{2} \div (-3)$

10. $\dfrac{5}{9} \div 1\dfrac{2}{3}$

11. $-4\dfrac{3}{4} \div \left(-1\dfrac{1}{4}\right)$

12. $-12\dfrac{3}{4} \div 4\dfrac{1}{4}$

13. $-3\dfrac{8}{9} \div \left(-1\dfrac{2}{3}\right)$

14. $8 \div \left(-2\dfrac{1}{2}\right)$

15. $6\dfrac{1}{3} \div 1\dfrac{2}{3}$

Answer Choices

$-\dfrac{1}{2}$ **S**	$-\dfrac{3}{4}$ **F**	$-1\dfrac{1}{3}$ **U**	$-3\dfrac{1}{5}$ **I**	$-2\dfrac{2}{3}$ **R**	$\dfrac{5}{8}$ **E**
$3\dfrac{4}{5}$ **O**	$-\dfrac{9}{20}$ **P**	$1\dfrac{1}{2}$ **A**	$\dfrac{1}{3}$ **T**	$2\dfrac{1}{3}$ **G**	-3 **H**
$-\dfrac{2}{3}$ **N**	$-1\dfrac{1}{2}$ **K**				

___ ___ ___ ___ ___ ___ ___ ___ ___ ___ ___ ___ ___ ___
10 12   6   7   4   11   5   1   15   2   8   14   3   13   9

8.4 Gravity

This English mathematician and scientist discovered the principles of gravity. Who was he?

To answer the question, find the quotients. Simplify, if necessary. Match each answer to one of the answer choices in the list after the problems. Then write the letter that corresponds to each answer in the space above its problem number at the bottom of the page. Some answers will be used more than once. Some answers will not be used.

1. $\frac{3}{5} \div \left(-\frac{2}{3}\right)$ 2. $-\frac{1}{4} \div \left(-\frac{1}{2}\right)$ 3. $-\frac{1}{4} \div \frac{1}{10}$ 4. $\frac{1}{12} \div \left(-\frac{1}{6}\right)$ 5. $\frac{3}{5} \div \left(-\frac{9}{10}\right)$

6. $1\frac{2}{3} \div \frac{2}{3}$ 7. $\frac{2}{5} \div \left(-\frac{4}{5}\right)$ 8. $-5\frac{1}{4} \div 7$ 9. $0 \div \left(-\frac{3}{4}\right)$ 10. $8 \div \left(-3\frac{1}{5}\right)$

11. $1\frac{1}{8} \div \left(-1\frac{1}{2}\right)$ 12. $5\frac{1}{4} \div 4\frac{3}{8}$ 13. $-5\frac{5}{6} \div 1\frac{1}{6}$ 14. $1\frac{4}{5} \div 3\frac{3}{5}$

Answer Choices

$\frac{3}{4}$ L $-\frac{1}{2}$ I $-\frac{2}{3}$ E $-\frac{9}{10}$ W $\frac{1}{2}$ N $-\frac{3}{4}$ S

$-2\frac{1}{2}$ A $1\frac{1}{5}$ T $1\frac{1}{9}$ J $2\frac{1}{2}$ C -5 R 0 O

$\overline{}$ $\overline{}$ $\overline{}$ $\overline{}$ $\overline{}$ $\overline{}$ $\overline{}$ $\overline{}$ $\overline{}$ $\overline{}$ $\overline{}$ $\overline{}$ $\overline{}$ $\overline{}$
 8   7   13   4   11   3   10   6   14   5   1   12   9   2

Dividing Signed Numbers

Evaluating Rational Numbers with Exponents

When evaluating rational numbers with exponents, you must simplify the exponents first. Then simplify the fractions.

Follow these guidelines:

- If the signs of the numbers are the same, the sign of the quotient is positive.

- If the signs of the numbers are different, the sign of the quotient is negative.

- If zero is divided by any number, the quotient is zero.

- Any number divided by zero is undefined.

$$\frac{-3^2}{2^3}$$ Simplify the exponents. $-3^2 = -(3 \times 3) = -9$ and $2^3 = 2 \times 2 \times 2 = 8$

$$\frac{-9}{8} = -1\frac{1}{8}$$ Simplify the fraction. Because the numerator is negative and the denominator is positive, the sign of the simplified fraction is negative.

Here is another example.

$$\frac{(-4)^2}{2^2}$$ Simplify the exponents, then simplify the fraction.
$(-4)^2 = -4 \times (-4) = 16$ and $2^2 = 2 \times 2 = 4$

$$\frac{16}{4} = 4$$ Because the signs of the numerator and the denominator are the same, the sign of the whole number is positive.

Here are more examples.

$$\frac{(-7)^2}{-6^2} = \frac{-7 \times (-7)}{-(6 \times 6)} = \frac{49}{-36} = -1\frac{13}{36} \qquad \frac{(-2)^3}{2^2} = \frac{-2 \times (-2) \times (-2)}{2 \times 2} = \frac{-8}{4} = -2$$

Practice
Evaluate the following.

1. $\frac{-2^2}{4^2}$ 2. $\frac{-5^3}{(-9)^2}$ 3. $\frac{-3^3}{4^2}$ 4. $\frac{6^2}{4^2}$ 5. $\frac{-8^2}{(-3)^4}$

Dividing Signed Numbers

© Judith A. Muschla and Gary Robert Muschla

8.5 Wyoming

The name Wyoming comes from a Delaware Indian word. What was the original meaning of this word?

To answer the question, evaluate the rational numbers and their exponents. Match each answer to one of the answer choices in the list after the problems. Then write the letter that corresponds to each answer in the space above its problem number at the bottom of the page. One answer will not be used.

1. $\dfrac{2^3}{-6^2}$ 2. $\dfrac{-4^2}{-2^2}$ 3. $\dfrac{(-7)^2}{-7^2}$ 4. $\dfrac{3^2}{-2^4}$ 5. $\dfrac{-2^5}{3^0}$

6. $\dfrac{-5^2}{(-5)^3}$ 7. $\dfrac{-1^2}{3^2}$ 8. $\dfrac{(-4)^2}{(-2)^3}$ 9. $\dfrac{4^3}{-2^4}$ 10. $\dfrac{(-9^2)}{6^2}$

11. $\dfrac{(-8)^2}{(-2)^6}$ 12. $\dfrac{3^3}{-6^2}$ 13. $\dfrac{-5}{(-5)^2}$ 14. $\dfrac{10^3}{10^2}$ 15. $\dfrac{-3^4}{(-2)^5}$

Answer Choices

$-\dfrac{1}{9}$ **U**   1 **E** $-\dfrac{9}{16}$ **G** $-\dfrac{1}{5}$ **I** -2 **Y** $-\dfrac{3}{4}$ **V** $-\dfrac{2}{9}$ **A**

-32 **S**   10 **M**   4 **D** $2\dfrac{17}{32}$ **N** $\dfrac{1}{5}$ **R** -1 **T** $1\dfrac{1}{2}$ **P**

-4 **O** $2\dfrac{1}{4}$ **L**

___ ___ ___ ___ ___ ___ ___ ___ ___   ___ ___ ___
14   9   7   15   3   1   13   15   5   1   15   2

___ ___ ___ ___ ___ ___ ___   ___ ___ ___ ___ ___ ___ ___ ___ ___ ___
12   1   10   10   11   8   5   1   10   3   11   6   15   1   3   13   15   4

8.6 Review: Developers of a System of Mathematics

These people developed a system of mathematics about 4,000 years ago. Who were they?

To answer the question, decide if the answers to the problems are correct. If the given answer is correct, write the letter for **correct** in the space above the problem's number at the bottom of the page. If the answer is incorrect, write the letter for **incorrect**.

1. $-45 \div (-9) = 5$

2. $-64 \div 8 = -8$

3. $0 \div (-12) = -12$

I. correct	**N.** correct	**H.** correct
E. incorrect	**S.** incorrect	**A.** incorrect

4. $-\dfrac{1}{2} \div 3 = -\dfrac{1}{6}$

5. $\dfrac{8}{15} \div \left(-\dfrac{4}{5}\right) = \dfrac{2}{3}$

6. $-1 \div 2\dfrac{1}{2} = -\dfrac{2}{5}$

S. correct	**N.** correct	**Y.** correct
E. incorrect	**A.** incorrect	**C.** incorrect

7. $-\dfrac{3}{4} \div 1\dfrac{7}{8} = -1\dfrac{13}{32}$

8. $-5\dfrac{1}{4} \div \left(-\dfrac{1}{4}\right) = -4\dfrac{1}{5}$

9. $-7\dfrac{1}{2} \div 2\dfrac{1}{2} = 3$

I. correct	**E.** correct	**T.** correct
N. incorrect	**B.** incorrect	**B.** incorrect

10. $\dfrac{(-2)^4}{-3^2} = 3\dfrac{5}{9}$

11. $\dfrac{-4^2}{(-5)^2} = -\dfrac{16}{25}$

H. correct	**O.** correct
L. incorrect	**J.** incorrect

__ __ __ __ __ __ __ __ __ __ __
9 3 8 6 10 11 7 1 5 2 4

Answer Key

Part 1

Multiplication Facts: 1. 27 2. 42 3. 15 4. 16 5. 16 6. 36 7. 60 8. 0

1.1 1. R 2. O 3. N 4. G 5. C 6. T 7. A 8. T 9. I 10. E 11. U 12. H 13. F 14. N
15. O 16. T
The Art of Counting

Multiples, Common Multiples, and Least Common Multiples: 1. First
10 multiples of 4: 4, 8, 12, 16, 20, 24, 28, 32, 36, 40; first 10 multiples of 6: 6,
12, 18, 24, 30, 36, 42, 48, 54, 60 2. First three common multiples of 4 and 6:
12, 24, 36; least common multiple of 4 and 6: 12

1.2 Note: For incorrect problems, correct answers are in parentheses. 1. E
2. O (The least common multiple is 6.) 3. I (25 is not a common multiple.)
4. E 5. K 6. M (45 is not a common multiple.) 7. S 8. Y 9. M (4, 8, 12, 16,
and 20 are the first five multiples of 4.) 10. U 11. C (0 is not a multiple of any
number.)
Mickey Mouse

Properties of Multiplication: 1. Associative 2. Property of 0 3. Commutative
4. Distributive 5. Property of 1

1.3 1. E 2. E 3. R 4. G 5. N 6. M 7. O 8. N 9. U 10. A
meganeuron

Multiplying by One-Digit Numbers: 1. 200 2. 570 3. 2,024 4. 13,210
5. 142,824

1.4 1. H 2. E 3. T 4. S 5. E 6. P 7. T 8. P 9. I 10. H 11. D 12. W 13. L 14. F
15. O
People of the South Wind

Multiplying by 10, 100, or 1,000: 1. 450 2. 870 3. 37,500 4. 69,200 5. 735,000

1.5   1. G 2. D 3. C 4. A 5. U 6. S 7. V 8. I 9. X 10. L 11. T 12. J 13. E
executive, legislative, judicial

Multiplying by Multiples of 10, 100, or 1,000: 1. 2,820 2. 20,000 3. 156,600 4. 528,000 5. 37,805,000

1.6   1. E 2. A 3. T 4. H 5. D 6. R 7. S 8. G 9. N 10. Y 11. F 12. O 13. W 14. L
Henry Wadsworth Longfellow

Multiplying by Two-Digit Numbers: 1. 6,507 2. 2,850 3. 7,056 4. 11,554 5. 21,045

1.7   1. E 2. I 3. S 4. E 5. M 6. V 7. N 8. R 9. K 10. X 11. O 12. F 13. L 14. O 15. W
mink, foxes, wolverines

1.8   Note: For incorrect problems, correct answers are in parentheses. 1. I (4,650) 2. E (4,136) 3. I 4. A 5. L 6. L (7,875) 7. D 8. O (18,096) 9. F 10. R (56,990) 11. L (13,234) 12. R (16,744) 13. M 14. L 15. M (367,470)
Millard Fillmore

1.9   1. R 2. A 3. S 4. A 5. S 6. E 7. A 8. I 9. N 10. I 11. O 12. P 13. L 14. U 15. H
Louisiana parishes

Multiplying by Two-, Three-, and Four-Digit Numbers: 1. 142,590 2. 70,320 3. 338,850 4. 1,631,772 5. 21,606,567

1.10   1. G 2. H 3. E 4. A 5. E 6. R 7. R 8. O 9. Y 10. O 11. F 12. T 13. F 14. M 15. T
Father of Geometry

1.11   1. U 2. R 3. E 4. G 5. I 6. C 7. T 8. H 9. A 10. V 11. N 12. S 13. L
largest living structure in the sea

1.12   Note: For incorrect problems, correct answers are in parentheses. 1. O (20,910) 2. A 3. O (24,192) 4. F (12,216) 5. S 6. T (157,685) 7. E 8. S 9. F (150,420) 10. E 11. W 12. F (2,578,165) 13. R (4,279,192) 14. L
Feast of Flowers

1.13   Note: For incorrect problems, correct answers are in parentheses. 1. R (8,568) 2. R (38,304) 3. I 4. T (57,546) 5. E 6. C 7. C 8. I (431,748) 9. N (588,072) 10. L 11. T (9,912,780) 12. C (21,160,759) 13. A 14. C 15. A (88,235,856)
Antarctic Circle

Estimating Products: 1. 2,720; 2,700 2. 34,916; 32,000 3. 16,511; 18,000 4. 103,085; 120,000 5. 300,872; 300,000

1.14 1. E 2. D 3. F 4. G 5. H 6. U 7. I 8. O 9. M 10. A 11. S 12. L 13. N 14. T
land of the midnight sun

Exponents: 1. 1,000 2. 36 3. 1 4. 81 5. 7

1.15 1. I 2. O 3. H 4. N 5. L 6. E 7. C 8. W 9. R 10. T 11. E 12. P
The Triple Crown

1.16 1. A 2. Y 3. G 4. I 5. D 6. S 7. U 8. L 9. W 10. R 11. M 12. C 13. B 14. N
running, bicycling, and swimming

Part 2

Basic Division Facts: 1. 9 2. 3 3. 8 4. 8 5. 3

2.1 1. N 2. S 3. S 4. D 5. A 6. M 7. A 8. N 9. A 10. T 11. A 12. I 13. L 14. P 15. L
plants and animals

Factors, Common Factors, and Greatest Common Factors: 1. Factors of 4: 1, 2, 4; Factors of 10: 1, 2, 5, 10; GCF of 4 and 10: 2 2. Factors of 9: 1, 3, 9; Factors of 36: 1, 2, 3, 4, 6, 9, 12, 18, 36; GCF of 9 and 36: 9 3. Factors of 14: 1, 2, 7, 14; Factors of 30: 1, 2, 3, 5, 6, 10, 15, 30; GCF of 14 and 30: 2 4. Factors of 16: 1, 2, 4, 8, 16; Factors of 28: 1, 2, 4, 7, 14, 28; GCF of 16 and 28: 4 5. Factors of 21: 1, 3, 7, 21; Factors of 27: 1, 3, 9, 27; GCF of 21 and 27: 3

2.2 Note: For incorrect problems, correct answers are in parentheses. 1. O (1, 2, 11, 22) 2. O 3. R (1, 2, 3, 4, 6, 12) 4. E (7) 5. D (1, 2, 3, 5, 6, 10, 15, 30) 6. W 7. Y 8. R (1, 5) 9. H 10. P
hydropower

Prime Numbers, Composite Numbers, and Prime Factorization: 1. 3 × 5 2. 2 × 5 3. 5 × 5 4. 2 × 2 × 2 × 3 5. 2 × 3 × 5

2.3 Note: For incorrect problems, correct answers are in parentheses.
1. A (prime) 2. O 3. O 4. E 5. R (Composite; 2 and 16 are a pair of factors.) 6. A (2 × 2 × 3 × 3) 7. J 8. P (2 × 2 × 2 × 7) 9. C (Composite; 7 and 13 are a pair of factors.) 10. D 11. B (2 and 3 are the prime factors of 12.)
Cape Bojador

Dividing Whole Numbers by One-Digit Divisors: 1. 23 2. 17 3. 50 R7
4. 422 5. 5,090 R5

2.4 1. S 2. A 3. E 4. I 5. E 6. R 7. O 8. D 9. N 10. L 11. G 12. D 13. G 14. D
15. C
dog sledding race

2.5 1. U 2. A 3. E 4. S 5. A 6. R 7. S 8. R 9. D 10. N 11. L 12. D 13. T 14. T
15. G
grassland, desert, tundra

Dividing Whole Numbers by 10 or 100: 1. 45 R6 2. 79 R8 3. 63 R94
4. 38 R92 5. 749 R38

2.6 1. A 2. O 3. T 4. T 5. R 6. N 7. N 8. O 9. Y 10. C 11. I 12. B 13. U 14. P
15. F
your carbon footprint

Dividing Whole Numbers by Multiples of 10 and 100: 1. 24 R18
2. 25 R4 3. 34 R28 4. 187 R2 5. 53 R359

2.7 1. M 2. S 3. I 4. K 5. O 6. E 7. A 8. I 9. T 10. O 11. L 12. R 13. P 14. Y
15. N
Yosemite National Park

Dividing Whole Numbers by Two-Digit Divisors: 1. 4 2. 6 R15
3. 123 R25 4. 50 R33 5. 59 R25

2.8 1. U 2. S 3. I 4. Y 5. T 6. A 7. I 8. D 9. R 10. I 11. G 12. R 13. R 14. F 15. N
grains, fruits, dairy

2.9 1. A 2. D 3. W 4. E 5. N 6. U 7. E 8. L 9. U 10. Y 11. I 12. H 13. O 14. Y
15. D
Huey, Dewey, and Louie

2.10 1. E 2. N 3. I 4. D 5. O 6. T 7. Z 8. M 9. U 10. X 11. W 12. C 13. H 14. A
15. R
Arizona, New Mexico, and Utah

Dividing Whole Numbers by Two- and Three-Digit Divisors:
1. 89 R50 2. 224 R18 3. 516 R62 4. 433 R36 5. 151 R35

2.11 1. O 2. O 3. E 4. E 5. D 6. R 7. W 8. K 9. O 10. P 11. Y 12. C 13. W 14. O
15. D
Woody Woodpecker

2.12 1. D 2. M 3. I 4. U 5. N 6. H 7. O 8. R 9. S 10. L 11. T 12. C 13. E 14. P
15. A
The Northern Mariana Islands and Puerto Rico

2.13 1. O 2. S 3. I 4. I 5. L 6. H 7. L 8. E 9. H 10. R 11. T 12. G 13. F 14. T
15. B
The Bill of Rights

2.14 1. T 2. N 3. S 4. R 5. B 6. L 7. H 8. I 9. P 10. F 11. A 12. E 13. M 14. D
amphibians, fish, and reptiles

2.15 1. V 2. N 3. I 4. A 5. O 6. H 7. S 8. R 9. F 10. T 11. E
The Sieve of Eratosthenes

Estimating Quotients: 1. 80 2. 10 3. 500 4. 400 5. 400

2.16 1. A 2. A 3. A 4. R 5. A 6. R 7. H 8. I 9. A 10. C 11. S 12. F
Sahara, Africa

Divisibility Rules: 1. yes 2. yes 3. no 4. no 5. yes

2.17 Note: For incorrect problems, correct answers are in parentheses. 1. N (4,275
is not divisible by 2.) 2. G (Numbers ending in 5 are not divisible by 10.)
3. A 4. O 5. O 6. L (19, for example, is not divisible by 9.) 7. T 8. O (28, for
example, is divisible by 4 but not by 8.) 9. P (It is not divisible by 4.) 10. L
paleontology

Finding Averages of Whole Numbers: 1. 40 2. 105 3. 202

2.18 1. N 2. R 3. S 4. E 5. O 6. H 7. F 8. T 9. M 10. J
Thomas Jefferson

2.19 1. C 2. T 3. O 4. R 5. M 6. S 7. E 8. P 9. Y 10. H
psychrometer

Part 3

Multiplying Whole Numbers and Decimals: 1. 6.3 2. 264.6 3. 85.28
4. 126.556 5. 22,797.6

3.1 1. I 2. P 3. A 4. N 5. N 6. U 7. T 8. C 9. E 10. T 11. R 12. S 13. O 14. F 15. O
sun protection factor

3.2 1. O 2. S 3. D 4. T 5. A 6. I 7. U 8. R 9. L 10. V 11. H 12. M 13. N 14. E
seven thousand nine hundred miles

Multiplying a Decimal by 10, 100, or 1,000: 1. 74.3 2. 420 3. 8,670
4. 6,021 5. 73,850

3.3 Note: For incorrect problems, correct answers are in parentheses. 1. L (79) 2. I
3. I 4. E 5. R (4,600) 6. S 7. R (3,040) 8. O (623.5) 9. N 10. N 11. T (39,600)
12. N 13. H (20.61) 14. A (790) 15. C
The Chronicles of Narnia

Multiplying Two Decimals: 1. 5.118 2. 0.00434 3. 0.85 4. 21.762 5. 10.15831

3.4 Note: For incorrect problems, correct answers are in parentheses. 1. A 2. I 3. E
(0.2993) 4. L 5. U (0.0288) 6. M (0.1952) 7. J 8. P (14.592) 9. N 10. Y 11. A
(9.135) 12. R (15.6672)
April, May, June

3.5 1. I 2. D 3. C 4. E 5. R 6. E 7. R 8. A 9. N 10. H 11. L 12. O 13. V 14. B
15. L
Orville Redenbacher

3.6 1. E 2. C 3. A 4. L 5. E 6. R 7. D 8. L 9. R 10. X 11. F 12. T 13. Y 14. H
15. H
Farley Drexel Hatcher

3.7 1. H 2. O 3. E 4. M 5. J 6. C 7. E 8. D 9. N 10. L 11. W 12. N 13. A 14. Y
15. I
Wendy, John, Michael

3.8 1. I 2. N 3. E 4. U 5. I 6. H 7. O 8. R 9. T 10. R 11. S 12. L 13. Y 14. T
15. A
The Louisiana Territory

3.9 1. M 2. I 3. D 4. T 5. K 6. N 7. E 8. O 9. L 10. R 11. A 12. H 13. Z 14. P
15. W
The Wizard of Menlo Park

Estimating Decimal Products: 1. 3.936; 5 2. 26.052; 30 3. 0.7128; 1
4. 2,575.93; 2,400 5. 36,088.098; 36,000

3.10 1. I 2. E 3. E 4. N 5. S 6. O 7. S 8. U 9. V 10. R 11. L 12. T 13. B 14. O
15. R
Robert Louis Stevenson

3.11 1. A 2. E 3. N 4. E 5. R 6. T 7. O 8. G 9. H 10. O 11. S 12. W 13. F 14. C
15. L
Town of the Large Canoes

Part 4

Dividing a Decimal by a One-Digit Whole Number: 1. 2.3 2. 0.51
3. 0.169 4. 9.01 5. 0.00812

4.1 1. E 2. U 3. R 4. E 5. L 6. O 7. L 8. T 9. S 10. A 11. D 12. A 13. N 14. G
15. B
Douglas Englebart

4.2 1. E 2. A 3. N 4. S 5. D 6. A 7. Y 8. T 9. N 10. R 11. C 12. I 13. O 14. B
15. F
strained baby food in a can

Dividing a Decimal by 10, 100, or 1,000: 1. 0.42 2. 0.0314 3. 0.0865
4. 30.02 5. 0.05187

4.3 1. E 2. A 3. I 4. E 5. A 6. S 7. N 8. T 9. R 10. A 11. C 12. V 13. N 14. I
15. M
Native Americans

Dividing a Decimal by a Two- or Three-Digit Whole Number: 1. 1.9
2. 0.43 3. 0.75 4. 0.019 5. 1.34

4.4 1. E 2. R 3. T 4. E 5. E 6. U 7. K 8. S 9. S 10. H 11. F 12. A 13. H 14. O
15. P
Speaker of the House

4.5 1. O 2. S 3. A 4. R 5. G 6. N 7. E 8. D 9. P 10. L 11. I 12. K 13. E 14. T
15. V
Everglades National Park

Dividing a Decimal by a Decimal: 1. 4.8 2. 6.6 3. 4.7 4. 2.74 5. 1.2

4.6 1. S 2. O 3. A 4. M 5. I 6. V 7. T 8. L 9. I 10. Y 11. N 12. R 13. P 14. W
15. E
Williamsport, Pennsylvania

4.7 1. R 2. M 3. N 4. H 5. R 6. O 7. A 8. L 9. A 10. I 11. W 12. I 13. S 14. Y
15. E
William Henry Harrison

4.8 1. F 2. O 3. N 4. R 5. U 6. S 7. T 8. Y 9. O 10. E 11. S 12. A 13. Q 14. M
15. C
Mary, Queen of Scots

4.9 1. F 2. R 3. U 4. I 5. P 6. I 7. N 8. R 9. E 10. B 11. O 12. S 13. T 14. E 15. M
Tribe of Superior Men

Estimating Decimal Quotients: 1. 3.4; 3 2. 2.35; 2 3. 75; 70 4. 5.1; 5 5. 1.8; 2

4.10 1. I 2. A 3. A 4. L 5. A 6. M 7. S 8. L 9. S 10. V 11. N 12. L 13. K 14. S 15. L
Smallville, Kansas

Decimal Quotients That Repeat: 1. $1.5\overline{7}$ 2. $0.9\overline{3}$ 3. $5.1\overline{3}$ 4. $17.\overline{6}$ 5. $9.\overline{6}$

4.11 1. S 2. R 3. E 4. O 5. N 6. Y 7. A 8. O 9. T 10. V 11. A 12. D 13. G 14. H 15. M
heavens to mergatroyd

4.12 1. M 2. E 3. R 4. I 5. D 6. H 7. S 8. R 9. U 10. E 11. N 12. L 13. U 14. O 15. P
one hundred miles per hour

4.13 1. Y 2. C 3. N 4. E 5. K 6. B 7. U 8. R 9. D 10. H
Huckleberry Hound

Part 5

Simplifying Fractions: 1. $\frac{4}{5}$ 2. $\frac{9}{10}$ 3. $\frac{3}{10}$ 4. $3\frac{3}{4}$ 5. $16\frac{7}{9}$

5.1 1. O 2. N 3. E 4. I 5. L 6. T 7. N 8. D 9. S 10. I 11. A 12. L 13. R 14. C 15. F
landfills and incinerators

Renaming Mixed Numbers as Improper Fractions and Improper Fractions as Mixed Numbers: 1. $\frac{15}{4}$ 2. $3\frac{1}{7}$ 3. $\frac{22}{5}$ 4. $3\frac{3}{5}$ 5. 8

5.2 1. A 2. C 3. R 4. W 5. K 6. I 7. B 8. G 9. H 10. E
Greek, Arabic, Hebrew

Multiplying Whole Numbers and Fractions: 1. $5\frac{1}{3}$ 2. $3\frac{3}{8}$ 3. $3\frac{3}{5}$ 4. 2 5. $2\frac{1}{3}$

5.3 1. N 2. H 3. E 4. A 5. T 6. W 7. T 8. L 9. G 10. S 11. I 12. S 13. K 14. L 15. R
starlight twinkles

Multiplying Simple Fractions: 1. $\frac{3}{8}$ 2. $\frac{5}{12}$ 3. $\frac{4}{15}$ 4. $\frac{5}{18}$ 5. $\frac{1}{3}$

5.4 1. F 2. T 3. L 4. E 5. C 6. R 7. A 8. S 9. I 10. P 11. H 12. W 13. O 14. D 15. B
Oswald Chesterfield Cobblepot

5.5 1. A 2. R 3. S 4. L 5. I 6. R 7. N 8. E 9. L 10. O 11. T 12. F 13. E 14. V 15. K
Franklin Roosevelt

Multiplying Fractions and Mixed Numbers: 1. $\frac{7}{18}$ 2. $1\frac{7}{8}$ 3. $3\frac{1}{15}$ 4. $1\frac{5}{8}$ 5. $2\frac{11}{12}$

5.6 1. A 2. O 3. F 4. C 5. U 6. L 7. M 8. I 9. F 10. I 11. Y 12. L 13. B 14. W 15. D
William "Buffalo Bill" Cody

5.7 1. O 2. I 3. N 4. R 5. E 6. E 7. A 8. S 9. F 10. L 11. T 12. M 13. J 14. F 15. H
The Jefferson Memorial

Multiplying Mixed Numbers: 1. $7\frac{7}{8}$ 2. $4\frac{2}{3}$ 3. $3\frac{1}{2}$ 4. $5\frac{1}{4}$ 5. $15\frac{15}{16}$

5.8 1. O 2. E 3. L 4. E 5. R 6. D 7. L 8. A 9. S 10. K 11. S 12. G 13. W 14. N 15. Y
New York and Los Angeles

5.9 1. O 2. D 3. E 4. G 5. A 6. B 7. G 8. N 9. E 10. B 11. L 12. C 13. R 14. L 15. S
Scrabble and Boggle

5.10 1. C 2. M 3. N 4. L 5. C 6. E 7. N 8. U 9. B 10. T 11. A 12. R 13. U 14. R 15. S
translucent sea cucumber

Estimating the Products of Fractions: 1. $\frac{2}{3}$; 1 2. $1\frac{7}{12}$; 2 3. $3\frac{9}{10}$; 4 4. 34; 30 5. $11\frac{2}{3}$; 12

5.11 1. N 2. N 3. E 4. S 5. O 6. V 7. E 8. U 9. P 10. E 11. D 12. L
eleven pounds

5.12 Note: For incorrect problems, correct answers are in parentheses. 1. E
2. E $\left(21\frac{1}{2}\right)$ 3. I $\left(\frac{31}{4}\right)$ 4. L 5. T 6. T $\left(\frac{7}{8}\right)$ 7. C 8. X $\left(1\frac{7}{8}\right)$ 9. F $\left(5\frac{1}{2}\right)$ 10. A
Felix the Cat

Part 6

Dividing Whole Numbers and Fractions: 1. 3 2. 30 3. $\frac{3}{8}$ 4. 20 5. $\frac{4}{15}$

6.1 1. I 2. R 3. U 4. E 5. T 6. I 7. E 8. C 9. A 10. H 11. F 12. L 13. B 14. A
15. M
America the Beautiful

Dividing Simple Fractions: 1. $\frac{8}{9}$ 2. $1\frac{1}{2}$ 3. $\frac{3}{4}$ 4. $\frac{4}{5}$ 5. $1\frac{1}{4}$

6.2 1. D 2. G 3. T 4. S 5. I 6. E 7. A 8. R 9. L 10. I 11. N 12. O 13. A 14. H
15. W
isolated thing in water

6.3 1. I 2. U 3. A 4. E 5. D 6. V 7. I 8. E 9. M 10. L 11. T 12. R 13. Y 14. H
15. T
relative humidity

Dividing Fractions and Mixed Numbers: 1. $5\frac{1}{2}$ 2. 22 3. $\frac{8}{21}$ 4. $\frac{2}{17}$ 5. 10

6.4 1. O 2. A 3. S 4. H 5. B 6. R 7. A 8. T 9. E 10. G 11. N 12. D 13. Y 14. D
15. K
Yankees beat the Dodgers

6.5 1. R 2. E 3. I 4. P 5. H 6. O 7. R 8. T 9. L 10. R 11. H 12. M 13. Y 14. T
15. A
Hart Memorial Trophy

Dividing Mixed Numbers: 1. $3\frac{1}{2}$ 2. $1\frac{1}{4}$ 3. $1\frac{7}{8}$ 4. 1 5. $2\frac{4}{9}$

6.6 1. A 2. E 3. U 4. T 5. N 6. H 7. T 8. U 9. Y 10. O 11. K 12. B 13. C 14. S
15. D
Butte County, South Dakota

6.7 1. T 2. O 3. N 4. A 5. T 6. U 7. D 8. O 9. W 10. N 11. H 12. S 13. U 14. D
15. P
two thousand pounds

6.8 1. H 2. N 3. P 4. E 5. O 6. Y 7. N 8. E 9. D 10. L 11. D 12. A 13. T 14. A
15. K
donkey and elephant

Estimating Fraction Quotients: 1. $1\frac{11}{49}$; 1 2. $1\frac{9}{10}$; 2 3. $9\frac{13}{18}$; 9 4. $1\frac{3}{4}$; 2
5. $\frac{80}{81}$; 1

6.9 1. N 2. E 3. A 4. I 5. I 6. V 7. L 8. R 9. N 10. K 11. P 12. W
Rip Van Winkle

Simplifying Complex Fractions: 1. $\frac{1}{32}$ 2. 9 3. $3\frac{3}{8}$ 4. $\frac{3}{4}$ 5. $3\frac{1}{10}$

6.10 1. N 2. I 3. T 4. A 5. E 6. G 7. W 8. D 9. H 10. E 11. L 12. R 13. R 14. C
15. X
Alexander Cartwright

Expressing Fractions as Terminating or Repeating Decimals:
1. 0.6 2. 0.875 3. $0.\overline{5}$ 4. $0.\overline{18}$ 5. 3.5

6.11 1. I 2. O 3. A 4. H 5. D 6. N 7. V 8. T 9. L 10. S 11. E 12. G 13. B 14. R
beside the long tidal river

Changing Decimals to Fractions: 1. $\frac{3}{10}$ 2. $\frac{3}{4}$ 3. $2\frac{2}{5}$ 4. $\frac{1}{125}$ 5. $7\frac{23}{100}$

6.12 1. O 2. U 3. C 4. I 5. S 6. A 7. R 8. E 9. P 10. D 11. T 12. H 13. M 14. N
15. L
The National Aeronautics and Space Administration

6.13 Note: For incorrect problems, correct answers are in parentheses. 1. E (28)
2. I $\left(\frac{5}{6}\right)$ 3. S 4. A 5. D 6. H (12) 7. R $\left(\frac{5}{18}\right)$ 8. L 9. H 10. G (0.28)
Highlanders

Part 7

Multiplying Two Integers: 1. –18 2. 35 3. 12 4. 0 5. –32

7.1 1. E 2. I 3. U 4. A 5. K 6. C 7. L 8. H 9. A 10. L 11. T 12. S 13. T 14. A 15. Y
Salt Lake City, Utah

7.2 1. O 2. A 3. E 4. I 5. S 6. E 7. H 8. R 9. D 10. T 11. R 12. G 13. N 14. T 15. U
Gertie the Dinosaur

Multiplying More Than Two Integers: 1. 36 2. –12 3. 56 4. –64

7.3 1. I 2. U 3. A 4. E 5. T 6. G 7. D 8. R 9. C 10. O 11. B 12. N 13. P 14. S 15. W
brass, strings, percussion, woodwinds

Evaluating Integers with Exponents: 1. 16 2. 343 3. –25 4. 25 5. 8

7.4 1. T 2. P 3. N 4. R 5. D 6. S 7. M 8. W 9. O 10. A 11. H 12. Y 13. E 14. I 15. L
The Indianapolis Motor Speedway

Multiplying Two Rational Numbers: 1. $\frac{8}{15}$ 2. $-1\frac{1}{5}$ 3. $-3\frac{8}{9}$ 4. 10 5. $-4\frac{3}{8}$

7.5 1. N 2. D 3. O 4. Y 5. O 6. S 7. E 8. L 9. E 10. A 11. T 12. L 13. C 14. T 15. H
The Old Colony State

7.6 1. O 2. U 3. E 4. T 5. B 6. E 7. Y 8. P 9. L 10. P 11. R 12. R 13. D 14. S 15. W
Sweet Polly Purebred

7.7 Note: For incorrect problems, correct answers are in parentheses. 1. U 2. Y (64) 3. E (0) 4. Y (–42) 5. N 6. H 7. C (–1) 8. B $\left(\frac{5}{18}\right)$ 9. E 10. K $\left(-3\frac{1}{2}\right)$ 11. K 12. D

The Kentucky Derby

Part 8

Dividing Integers: 1. −4 2. 5 3. 2 4. −2 5. 6

8.1 1. U 2. N 3. I 4. O 5. E 6. T 7. R 8. A 9. H 10. F 11. Y 12. D 13. S 14. X
six thousand six hundred forty

8.2 1. O 2. A 3. R 4. S 5. T 6. Y 7. S 8. T 9. E 10. U 11. W 12. L 13. E 14. B
15. I
bitter, sour, salty, sweet

Dividing Rational Numbers: 1. $-\frac{1}{6}$ 2. $\frac{5}{6}$ 3. 2 4. $-2\frac{1}{2}$ 5. $-1\frac{3}{4}$

8.3 1. T 2. F 3. N 4. P 5. R 6. E 7. S 8. K 9. S 10. T 11. O 12. H 13. G 14. I
15. O
the sport of kings

8.4 1. W 2. N 3. A 4. I 5. E 6. C 7. I 8. S 9. O 10. A 11. S 12. T 13. R 14. N
Sir Isaac Newton

Evaluating Rational Numbers with Exponents: 1. $-\frac{1}{4}$ 2. $-1\frac{44}{81}$
3. $-1\frac{11}{16}$ 4. $2\frac{1}{4}$ 5. $-\frac{64}{81}$

8.5 1. A 2. D 3. T 4. G 5. S 6. R 7. U 8. Y 9. O 10. L 11. E 12. V 13. I 14. M
15. N
mountains and valleys alternating

8.6 Note: For incorrect problems, correct answers are in parentheses. 1. I
2. N 3. A (0) 4. S 5. A $\left(-\frac{2}{3}\right)$ 6. Y 7. N $\left(-\frac{2}{5}\right)$ 8. B (21) 9. B (−3)
10. L $\left(-1\frac{7}{9}\right)$ 11. O
Babylonians